LIFE IN THE SLOW LANE

Collected Pieces from Ten Years of Two-Lane Livin' Magazine

BY LISA HAYES-MINNEY

Forty of the pieces within were originally published in similar form in *Two-Lane Livin' Magazine*.

"Burdens and Blessings" was first published in *The Calhoun Chronicle*, shortly before *Two-Lane Livin'* was launched. The names of family members in that essay were represented by numbers—FM1, FM2, FM3. In this version, the names mentioned are completely fictitious.

Author Photo by Tamara Hough. Cover photo by Pedro Sandrini. Back cover photo by http://www.ForestWander.com.

ISBN-978-1-79473-493-7

For additional projects by this author, visit http://www.lhayesminney.net.

Dedication:

To my husband Frank, who has always supported my creative work, and spent ten years, in rain, hail, sleet, snow, road construction, flooding, high wind; behind school busses, tanker trucks, grandmas, and big rigs, day and night, delivering the magazine we produced. The decade I spent working from home producing the magazine was life in the slow lane for me—for Frank, it was not.

Also to the readers of *Two-Lane Livin' Magazine*, who waited anxiously for Frank to arrive, shared their copy with family and friends, and loved us all decade long.

Foreword

Anyone who wanted to know what life was like in rural central West Virginia during the late 1900s and early 2000s could turn to *Two Lane Livin' Magazine* each month and get a pretty accurate verbal photo of the landscape. All of the columnists for the magazine were West Virginians (or previous West Virginians) who lived or had lived in the rural regions of the Mountain State. It was NOT a publication which featured articles by writers from outside the region who came in and wrote about their reflections of Two-Lane Livin' after spending a few days driving the roads. The editor, Lisa Minney, lived on a farm in the very heart of central West Virginia. She had not just read about living on the Two Lanes, she experienced it.

When you opened the publication each month Lisa's reflections of living in rural West Virginia greeted you. She sort of set the standard for the other writers who contributed an article each month. She wrote about the scenery, dawns, and sunsets that she enjoyed each day. She told her readers about the ducks, geese, and aquatic life that inhabited the pond that was located near her house. The readers learned about her efforts in her garden. She shared her successes and her failures, often in great detail. Gardening was an enterprise with which all of the readers could identify.

Some of her columns discussed the trials and tribulations of living in the rural, sometimes isolated, areas of West Virginia. But mostly she ballyhooed the joys and serenity of rural living. While readers read about the hazards of driving the two-lane roads when they were covered with snow and ice, they also read about the under-reported joy of the splendor that the autumn months always brought to West Virginia. Everyone enjoyed reading about the old Subaru with ten million miles on it that Lisa used to deliver her papers each month. She wrote about adventures with which rural folks could identify.

Two-Lane Livin' fans also often got a view of Lisa's inner reflections on life itself from her columns. She probed areas that everybody ponders such as, am I living the life that I should be living, or should I be doing something else? She wrote about forks in the road that we all encounter, never quite knowing for sure which road to take. But those of us who knew her well knew she "took the one less traveled." Who among us has not had such thoughts? Yet she never sermonized. None of her columns ever told anyone how to live their life. There was no advice for the lovelorn.

There was never any local news in *Two Lane Livin' Magazine*. Lisa left that to the rural county newspapers. And she NEVER discussed national events nor did she allow any of her contributing writers to tackle controversial issues. She wanted articles that reflected the life of rural West Virginians (or rural folks just about anywhere) and she provided a perfect example each month in her own column. Readers enjoyed the positive outlook.

The immense popularity of the magazine was obvious. It was evidenced by the constant increase in the number which was published. But more than that, those of us who contributed a monthly column often got unsolicited comments from readers. As I traveled the state playing music and calling square dances, I heard high praise about the publication everywhere I went. Even today, some years after the magazine has ceased publication, I still get comments about it.

Those who have never seen a copy of *Two-Lane Livin' Magazine* should find this book refreshing. Those who have read some of Lisa's columns can take a nice trip again down memory lane.

Mack Samples
(Author of eleven books, Musician, Square Dance Caller, and former columnist for *Two-Lane Livin' Magazine.)*
2019

Introduction

From August 2007 through December 2017, my husband Frank and I produced *Two-Lane Livin' Magazine*, a free, monthly, tabloid-size, newsprint publication that presented regular columns and features related to rural, sustainable living. All of our columnists were volunteers who were passionate about an issue or topic or were storytellers highlighting the folklore and features of West Virginia.

When we decided to create and launch the magazine, I was desperate to leave my position as a small-town newspaper reporter. Though it was my dream job, after four years I found I could not separate my life from the job, and at that time, Frank and I were taking interest in simplifying our lives and making use of the land we lived on. Many of the original columnists of the magazine were people we personally sought out for advice on gardening, raising chickens and bees, simple living, budgeting, holistic health, and more. Once the magazine launched, columnists came to us, offering their unique perspectives and knowledge.

We had no idea if anyone would be interested in the magazine. Our original intention was to produce 8,000 monthly copies to deliver throughout an eight-county region. To our delight, every copy of the first issue was gone in three days. So, we increased the run of the second issue to 10,000 copies. Those were gone in a week. As time passed, and budget allowed, we continued to increase copies. By the end of our ten-year run, we were producing 18,000 monthly copies with Frank circulating copies into a 16-county region every month. We had subscribers in 14 states. We learned that folks passed their copies on to neighbors, mailed them to out-of-state family, shared them again and again. We estimate that we were reaching an average of 40,000 readers monthly. No matter what we did, we simply could not budget and produce enough copies to meet demand.

After ten years of working from home, farming, gardening, and distributing the magazine every month, our lives shifted again. I finished graduate school and began teaching and working outside the home. Frank also began taking on other projects. Life had sped up on us again, and we reached a point where we could no longer keep up with the garden or the magazine. We gave up both. We have two hens now in a chicken house that holds 30, and I grew a few tomatoes on the porch this year, a far cry from our peak garden year with more than 300 tomato plants. But we still have full jars in the pantry, fresh herbs, eggs, and honey. Though we no longer focus on farming, gardening, and homesteading, our decade spent producing our own food and our own magazine has had lasting effects on our reader's lives and our own lives.

We featured more than 35 columnists in *Two-Lane Livin' Magazine* over that decade, and my personal column, "Two-Lane for Life," appeared in all 123 issues. During my tenure as editor, publisher, and columnist for *Two-Lane Livin'*, I tried to learn about homesteading and farming from our columnists and my own research; apply the principles of sustainable, simple living to my own life; and share those experiences with our readers. Several of our columnists have compiled their work for the magazine into books, and I hope you will enjoy their collections as well as this assembly of some of my personal favorites from my own work in the magazine.

I'm grateful for the years we were able to get back to the land and produce our own food and our own publication. And though, in the end, we decided to return to the rat race, we will never lose the knowledge that we can sustain ourselves if we need to, and the principles of the simple living mindset will remain with us forever. I miss those days when we had morning coffee on the porch before heading to the garden, days when we had plenty of work to do, but nowhere we had to be. Though we still live amongst the two-lane roads, we hustle and bustle now.

Though it was hard work from dawn to dusk, I sure do miss life in the slow lane.

LHM, 2019

Table of Contents

GARDEN LIFE

Garden Servitude

If we are what we eat, then I am our garden. Eight months of the year I'm involved in tasks relating to the garden, two months of the year I'm planning or clearing the garden, and twelve months of the year, we're eating our garden harvest.

This will be our fifth year with a garden, and in many ways, I still feel like an amateur. So much trial and error. We don't have a system yet. We're still discovering lots of things that don't work, though we also have learned things that do.

We are also prone to order more, sow more, plant more, harvest more than we need or can handle. Already, seed trays are taking over the house, as they do each year this time. Water and dirt are maneuvered through the house, finding each sunny location available.

But there is no guarantee of success. Last year I purchased a mini greenhouse, which I forgot to open one warm morning and burned up all the seedlings. On the second try, I remembered to let it breathe on warm days, but then the spring winds blew the whole thing over and all was lost. We ordered 25 strawberry plants - all but three died. We try corn every year, with disappointing results. The only successful method we've found for rabbit control is to let the rabbit beagle loose in the garden. We still lose some plants during the ensuing chase, but not as many as the rabbit takes out.

But we keep trying. I've ordered more strawberry plants, corn seed, eggplant again. (The eggplant has never survived - not even to the blossom stage.) We're learning tricks of the trade -- row covers, compost tea, trellises, solar fence chargers and more. Still learning, and each year, we hope to do better.

We've had to do a lot of "do-overs." I didn't leave enough space in the perennial garden for the plants to spread, and when dividing them, I had no planned space to put them. The ended up here and there - only to become lunch for rabbits and deer, or to be destroyed by scratching hens.

Of course, we've done well with tomatoes, peas, green beans, peppers. We always plant enough that we can afford to lose a few. We've had both good and bad years for watermelon, squash, pumpkin, zucchini. We've learned NOT to plant more than we need of those, because even a bad year will likely produce too many.

I'm not sure why we can't seem to get a garden groove we click into every year as I imagine other, more experienced gardeners do. I think on this far too often, but I have come up with a theory. By far, the most difficult thing to learn about the garden is to work on its schedule. Gardeners are merely garden servants - resigning their lives to the demands of the garden. Plant by the moon, water in the morning, weed as needed, harvest when ready.

In the first year, we planted everything at one time. Peas withered and greens soured in the heat, melons never ripened before snowfall, tomatoes, and green beans all came on at one time, and it was impossible to get them all canned or frozen before they spoiled.

You must be prepared to flex with the weather, respond immediately to diseases and invaders, constantly maintain moisture levels, vigilantly hold weeds at bay.

You can't schedule a garden around your life. You must work your life around the needs of the garden. It is a difficult adjustment. I'm sure there's a way to plant a garden to where there could be scheduled breaks during the season, but the logistics of such are beyond me.

But even beyond that, you must be willing to relinquish. You must make a commitment to raise the garden like a child, to provide nurturing and care as needed -not when it's convenient. Sometimes it feels I am enslaved by it from April until October. Other times I cannot imagine how we could survive - physically, spiritually, financially - without it. Every time we make pizza, with the first bite I swear aloud that I make the best pizza sauce in the world. I smile each time I open a jar of tomato soup, I feel special knowing I have secret ingredients and special touches for the foods I create. Jars of ketchup are like fine wines - they taste different depending on that year's harvest.

This year, I am a little reluctant (but ready) to plant the seeds that will control my life for the next nine months and nurture our bodies for a year or more. I haven't yet finished my winter projects, and early planting is my sign that there's not much time left. Soon, if not finished, many of them will be put on the back burner until next winter. Some, I may never pick up again. Some, I'll have to pick at as time (and the garden) allows.

Usually, around this time, I am aching for the arrival of spring. But this year, I stand wondering where winter went. So, for March I'll scramble to get winter things done and try to keep planting and sowing in accordance with the planting calendar I get each year from the local extension office.

If you don't normally garden, try one garden-friendly project this year. Grow a tomato in a pot on the porch, stick some sweet potato starts in your potted plant arrangements, scatter wildflower seeds for honeybees, visit the local farmer's market. Find a way to connect to local food, and to your community's agricultural system. So many of us are still learning, and we could use all the help we can get.

Gardening: The Best Kind of Therapy

Right now, there's not a plant showing in the garden. All the beds have been turned and tilled, but only a quarter of them have been planted. Tiny seeds still underground, or barely peeking above. Of course, there are about 200 plants in the front room, just aching to get outside. I'd like to get them out there too but resisted the urge this past weekend knowing there's at least one more frost yet to come - maybe two.

I bought a row cover this year (our first) but I'm not sure I trust it. I stretched it out, looked at it, and decided it would be good for early lettuces, but I wasn't going to trust my heirloom tomatoes to it. And so, in the basement they wait with more plants, along with way too much seed.

We've been hoarding seed the past couple of years, and it is time to flush out the old and replenish the stock with new. So much carrot seed, cabbage seed and all kinds of peppers. One of the main themes of gardening is rotation: rotating crops, seeds, pantry, freezer. Anything that involves the garden has an expiring potency. Older seeds have a lower germination rate, so we plant the seed, knowing we'll have to figure what to do with the abundance at harvest time.

I know there are gardeners out there who plan the entire growing season, seed to harvest. Some have 20 years or more experience, so I try to be forgiving of our own "organic" (occurring or developing gradually and naturally, without being contrived) approach to "organic" (farm methods not using synthetic pesticides and chemical fertilizers) gardening.

After five years as gardeners, we're still learning. But one thing I have learned is that you can't plan a garden. Unless you can totally control the environment you grow in, you can never predict the outcome. Some years are good for peppers, others are good years for tomatoes or melons or root crops. Some years are great garden years. Some years are good for nothing.

I once saw a sign in someone's garden which said, "He who plants beneath the sod, shows he has a faith in God." A garden is certainly a leap of faith. A gardener has faith that a tiny seed will not only grow but will also feed him for the months, sometimes years, ahead. A gardener has faith that a small seed will be nurtured in the darkness of the earth, survive the elements of the sky, avoid serving as lunch or dinner for animals and insects, and become something that will nourish us.

Plant a seed, give it water and warmth of sunshine, and it will become--a fruit, a vegetable, a flower, an herb. But that plant is vulnerable, so it needs a gardener with faith. Faith that the earth is rich with nutrients and enriching minerals. Faith that the rains will be steadily quenching, not pounding and heavy, that the sun will provide an easy warmth and not scorching heat. Faith that animals and insects are kept at bay by establishing boundaries, careful planning, and gentle tending.

It takes faith -- and a heck of a lot of work! But I recently heard an experienced gardener speaking of the way his gardens tended him. I had to nod my head in agreement. I was not feeling in a gardening mood this year at all. No inclination whatsoever. But after what seemed like two Februaries in a row? On the first sunny weekend, I immediately grabbed a hoe and headed that way. I could not wait to break soil, move around, break a sweat in the sun. And at the end of the day, I felt ten times better, though my muscles ached. After several days, I was falling asleep the minute my head hit the pillows. Some call it Garden Therapy.

Horticulture Therapy is "the use of plants and gardens for human healing and rehabilitation." It is an ancient practice, but a rather new profession.

An increasingly large body of research attests to the unique values of gardening as a therapy for people with physical, mental, emotional, and social disabilities. Plants are non-discriminating and nonthreatening, so it doesn't matter how old or intelligent a person is; their race or religion. Plants will respond to anyone providing care. Studies show that success with plants can lead to successes in other aspects of our lives.

Many health care researchers and practitioners say that Ecotherapy (aka green therapy, nature therapy, earth-centered therapy), in general, can have regenerative powers, improving mood and easing anxiety, stress, and depression. A walk in the country reduced depression in 71% of participants of one European study. The researchers found that as little as five minutes in a natural setting - whether walking in a park or gardening - improves mood, self-esteem, and motivation.

They say, "gardening is cheaper than therapy and you get tomatoes." Usually, the cheaper option of any situation requires more work -- and the garden is no different. But experienced gardeners know that as they work in the garden, the garden works within them. You don't need a huge garden to reap the benefits. You can have a few tomatoes in pots on the porch if you want. Five minutes a day can do you, and the plant, a world of good.

Polished & Chipped

For most of winter and spring, I have beautifully manicured finger and toenails. It's a layover vanity from my city-slicker days when I worked as a beautician. Why keep toenails that are hidden beneath wool socks all winter? Because I know what is under those socks.

By spring, my nails have grown to their longest, and look their best for the entire year. Then, the planting season arrives.

Even the heaviest coat of nail enamel can't remain flawless if you use your hands and fingers to work the earth. And the enamel will crack and peel after you scrub and scratch the dirt our from beneath your nails. And toenails? That shiny finish just fades away when your feet slip out of your muddy garden clogs and plop right down in the mud.

By the time the vegetable and flower gardens are planted, any resemblance my hands had to those of my pampered city days are long gone.

I don't recall my grandmother ever wearing nail polish. When I think of her hands, I picture them peeling an apple with a stone-sharpened paring knife. I picture her hands as she sat stringing beans, rolling out noodle dough, stirring a pot with a wooden spoon, washing and drying dishes. I see hard hands guiding quilt patches through a sewing machine.

The nail polish of those days would never have held up through all that anyway. The time spent in water alone would have just eroded such a finish.

Me? I'm half gardener, half desk potato. I dislike gloves and love to feel the dirt break and crumble between my hands, but I also need a clean and polished atmosphere around my computer and paperwork. Sometimes it seems that this is the conflict of my life – the need to have my feet, and hands (polished nails and all) in both worlds.

I can walk out of the garden, take off my work clothes, shower, primp and put on a skirt – and manage the transition from dirt to desktop in a business meeting. But my hands will give me away every time. Spotty polish, scratches, even a chip I haven't filed out yet – these are the signs that I'm not a polished businesswoman every day of my life. If it were not for the "fast-dry" nail enamels available today, these hints of my secret life – on hands and knees in the dirt cursing weeds and cavorting with vegetables and flowers – would be constantly exposed.

Run into me during delivery week when I'm also covered head to toe in black ink smudges from handling thousands of issues of Two-Lane Livin' – and I could look much like a ragamuffin. Black hands, smudged face, blown hair, chipped fingernails, and if it's raining, muddy shoes. Even our white vehicles are covered in black smudged fingerprints.

Not the perfect picture of a professional, I know.

There's a saying though, "As is the garden, so is the gardener." And right now, our garden is more manicured than my nails. My social presentation might be a bit ragged around the edges, but the lettuce bed is beautiful, and the tomatoes are in bloom.

And I am realizing a growing admiration for hands that reflect hard work. My grandmother's hands. My full-time gardener friend's hands, with plain nails cut short and toned muscles that run from the fingertips to the shoulder. Dirty hands covered in grease or mud or any other dark sign of manual labor. Calloused hands that have spent a lifetime mastering a trade. Hands that have spent the day manipulating and creating much more than simple words pecked into a keyboard.

We should remember to respect hands that are dirty, just as much as those that are clean. Dirty hands are often a sign of hard work.

Playing Chicken

It all started when I visited a friend who had three or four hens and two small chicken tractors (mobile pens) that were maybe four feet wide, five feet long and four feet high. They were like little tents made from chicken wire; half-covered in two cut-open lawn size trash bags. Her hens laid their eggs in a hanging basket pot, hung from the central high point of the tractor. Their water bottles were vinegar bottles, with one top side cut open, the handle wired to the wall of the chicken tent. Every day she moved the tractor a little to give the hens fresh grass, and every evening let them out to roam for an hour or so before they went back in their pen at dusk.

I thought it was the most adorable thing I had ever seen, and... I then wanted hens of my own. My friend was more than happy to give me one of her no-longer-in-use chicken tractors she made, large enough for 6-8 hens. We loaded it into the back of my truck and I brought it home, announcing to Frank that I wanted hens, and could house up to eight of them. He groaned. We compromised on four.

At that point, I don't know a darn thing about chickens. Didn't know where to buy hens in the middle of summer, didn't know what they ate, what their needs were, how often they lay eggs, how much they poop. But we had neighbors who were overrun with yard foul, and I asked for "four hens that lay brown eggs." It didn't matter what breed they were, or how old they were, I didn't know anything about breeds or age or any of that. We came home with one black, one white, one red, and one peppered hen.

I named them all right off the bat. I looked forward to letting them out in the mornings and would set my lawn chair in the afternoon shade so I could watch the four ladies pluck around the side yard I had thrown a makeshift fence around with old safety fence. Within a short period of time, they were fat and happy. That winter, I ordered "The Complete Idiot's Guide to Raising Hens," and the next spring, I decided I wanted more.

Frank built a BIG chicken tractor. Not an adorable tent I could move myself. A huge framed coop covered with chicken wire, a metal roof, and a full-sized door. HE could move it; I needed the John Deere mower to move it. But at least he was getting on board with the hen idea. We purchased six-year-old leghorns from neighbors for a total of ten hens.

Now, I didn't realize that the first four hens were fat hens bred for egg laying and for meat. Leghorns are fit and trim and don't even give a fence a second look. Fat meat hens are too lazy to care what's on the other side of the fence, as long as there's plenty of food on their side. But Leghorns are adventurous. They're active. They're curious. They want to know what's on the other side of every fence they encounter. Want to see the view from the roof of the outbuilding, and from the back porch swing. Leghorns give fat meat hens the idea that the pickings are better on the other side of the fence. Then the fence is pointless.

When hens aren't busy tearing up every flower bed in your yard, they like to sun themselves by the door you use when you carry their feed from the house. When one of the nameless Leghorns up and died one day out of the blue - I wasn't that troubled. "They're livestock," I told myself, "and I'm a farm-girl now." Besides, there were five other hens that looked just like it tossing the mulch out of my lily bed right there.

Frank, being a farm-boy and a man, wasn't that bothered by torn up flower beds or poop on the porch. And I admit, since we get company so rarely, I spent more time trying to protect my flower and herb gardens than the porch. And then Pepper died. You know, the peppered hen of the original four. The Barred Rock hen I loved the most. I managed not to cry--barely. And when I saw someone post online that they had 20 Barred Rock hens for sale, Frank agreed we would build some kind of chicken containment come spring, and we decided we'd get five hens right then. He then came home with ten.

Well, since we were building containment in the spring, had regular orders for eggs, and two chicken tractors--I decided I'd get six fat, lazy meat-and-egg chicks last month. You know, in case grocery prices keep rising. I ended up with eight. They're adorable peeping from their washtub in the basement, though their pen needs daily cleaning and our beagle Daisy is not quite pleased with their indoor presence.

I've been pushing Frank lately for that promised chicken containment field. But I had that wifely feeling my nagging was battling my husband's selective hearing - until today when he came home and announced that he'd just bought thirteen more hens. I'm pretty sure the look he got from me made him quickly follow up with, "I'll start working on that containment field tomorrow."

So, apparently, we now own—what.... 39 hens? How did this happen? I've already posted the thirteen new ones for sale online. And, we're taking orders for eggs again as we eat egg salad sandwiches and deviled eggs for lunch. (Scrambled for breakfast and pickled with dinner.) And though I ordered chicks that all look alike so I couldn't name them or bond with them, alas, one looks different than the others. Her name is Ester. And I know that she, and none of the others, will ever be meat.

Lying Fallow

When it comes to farming and gardening, I have found that it is quite easy to overdo it. I have learned, truly, moderation is key. But baby chicks can be purchased in bulk, in fact, when ordering, you must purchase at least a dozen. One more tray of spring plants can produce another thirty or more pounds of tomatoes. One more row or seed packet of beans can double or triple the bushels of beans that need stringing in the fall.

A ten-year-old oregano patch can spread to cover more than eight square feet. Mature perennials need divided. Fences eventually need mending, spades sharpened, hives and pens need to be maintained.

All the projects I was so excited about ten years ago, I now know, are work. Work, and time. And though I knew back then and was not afraid of the work, I sorely underestimated the amount of time truly required.

Gardens, bees, chickens, fields, these things do not wait. They do not wait until you have time, do not wait until you are ready. Weeds need pulled, beans need picked, hay needs cut. Bees swarm. Eggs, water, and feed need to be dealt with more than once a day.

At one point, we had more than 30 chickens and planted more than 100 tomato plants and six rows of beans.

For two people? Insanity is what that is.

These days, my sewing machine is packed away, as are my crochet needles, my pressure canner. And though June is upon us, we have not planted a garden this year. The pantry is still filled with jars from previous years, and we still get near a dozen eggs a day from our small flock of aging hens. We have four beehives, but three of them are swarms we caught this spring.

We can certainly take a break from gardening this year, but it feels shameful to not have a garden. I feel shame, and I feel a loss. A loss of a chance to fill more jars, a loss of the mornings pulling weeds and smashing stink bugs. A loss not to wander out again in the evenings sweating in the late day sun and swatting at deer flies. In many ways, gardeners are slaves to their gardens--you weed and water when it is needed, pick and harvest when it's ready. But at the same time, a garden is nourishing, not just to the body, but to the soul. (In some ways, I feel like we're taking the summer off. Like we're cheating or being lazy.)

Of course, we still have asparagus, garlic, horseradish, mushrooms in the perennial beds, and thyme, oregano, lemon balm, sage, and chives in the herb garden.

Won't we miss fresh produce? I don't think so. I have learned that someone will inevitably grow too many cucumbers and squash and will bring some to the library or the local mom and pop store. Heirloom tomatoes will find their way to the local farmer's markets.

What will I do with the extra summer days that for the last ten years have been spent tilling and canning? I hope I don't waste it. I hope to work on other things, like moderation and maintenance. Where to store empty canning jars or tomato stakes not in use? Do we need all those plant trays? I'm going to sharpen my hoe before I ever use it again, and I'm going to spend more time in the back-porch swing, watching the grass grow.

So, this summer, our garden will be lying fallow, a term used to describe land tilled and plowed but left unseeded. Some farmers do this to raise the fertility in the soil. I wonder what lying fallow will do for us, the humans that tend the garden, what fertility might rise in our lives and souls--if any. Perhaps I will find a way to truly simplify my life. But it hasn't happened so far.

The Professional Porch Sitter's Union

"The most important people in your life are the ones you can picture sitting on a porch with." Unknown

In the mid-1800s, a well-known landscape gardener named Andrew Jackson Downing began writing about his vision of the American home — and how it could stand apart from English architecture. Many scholars consider Downing to be "The Father of American Landscape Architecture," and for the designer, the porch was key. Downing saw it as the link from the house to nature.

In our agrarian culture, the porch connected human control, in the form of the house, to nature and the wilderness outside it. In the cities and towns, it served as a transitional space between the privacy of the home to the public realm of the world.

Before air conditioning became common, the porch represented the American ideal of family. An outdoor living room, where the family could retire on the porch after the activities of a long day. In the evenings, the outdoor air provided a cool alternative to the stuffy indoor temperatures.

That's what our back porch is like, an outdoor living room. There's a lounge chair, a glider, a sitting table and of course, the porch swing. We read, sit, rest, pass time there. When we have company, that's where we entertain them. Away from the television, outside in the air, where laughter can flow out across the lake and the fields.

In winter months, when it is too cold to be outside, I miss the porch. I'll stand at the back door and take in the view, which is also cold and stale in the winter season. But as soon as warmer temps come closer, I'll start sweeping and cleaning the porch and shaking the dust off the covers. My favorite room in the house isn't actually IN the house.

Imagine my surprise when I discovered the Professional Porch Sitters Union. Lifelong porch-sitter Claude Stephens of Louisville, Ky., founded the Professional Porch Sitters Union in 1999 after a long workday.

"It was tongue in cheek," Stephens, 50, says about the Professional Porch Sitters Union, an unorganized organization whose only objective is to get people to slow down and relax. The group's motto: "Sit down a spell. That can wait."

Stephens and his wife, Erin Henle, have perfected the art of porch sitting. They bring their tube radio onto their porch and listen as they play Scrabble and cards. When the weather cooperates, they eat their meals on the porch, which is furnished with a mishmash of hand-me-down comfortable chairs, tables, and a metal glider. Neighbors show up bearing garden produce and eager to discuss the world's problems.

"We're all too busy," Stephens says, as he relaxes and expounds on the joys of porches. "Our lives have become incredibly jammed with too much stuff. The porch is a place to slow down, sit back and just tell stories that celebrate our triumphs. It's a place to just be."

I decided to establish our own Professional Porch Sitters Union, Local Number 2. The official rules are just fine with me: no dues, no agendas, no Rules, no Regulations, no committees, no mailings, no membership requirements, no scheduled meetings, no meeting minutes. Meetings can be called by any member at any time. Attendance is optional.

Our local porch sitters union meets on a regular basis. Sometimes we meet on our porch, often on someone else's porch. Some folks have Adirondack chairs, others have deluxe porch swings with cup holders in the armrests. Some folks have indoor-outdoor carpet and others have chimineas or small fire pits where they roast hot dogs and toast marshmallows on a regular basis.

I cannot imagine living in the country without a usable, comfortable porch. It's a place for winding down, for stepping away from all the electronics and devices. It is a place to relax and chat and enjoy life, watching the grass grow or the world go by. The porch is a part of living in the natural world.

I have spent hours on our porch with another in comfortable silence. I've spent hours on a porch laughing. I've slept on our porch, worked, written, sang. I exercise there on warm mornings and we cuddle there on cool nights. Our porch carries nearly all the character of our home, it is the 'room' I think of when I think of home.

Is your porch a special place? Make it one and make use of it!

The Farmer's Market - Much More Than Produce

Question: What do the following items have in common? Honey, Wooden Spoons, Home-made Bread, Jewelry, Art, Potted House Plants, Granola, Make-Your-Own Laundry Soap Kits.

Answer: They are all available at the Farmer's Market.

Now, before I first visited the market years ago, when I pictured "Farmer's Market" in my mind, I pictured tables and/or truck beds of produce. But I discovered is that my mind's picture lacked the real detail and depth of what a Farmer's Market really is.

Every market is different. Depending on the location, the administrative structure, the vendors, the shoppers -- every market has its own unique value, personality, and features. And not only is every market different, but every market DAY is also different. Some markets have raffles, speakers, demonstrations. I've seen knife sharpening wheels in action, missed a canning lesson, had a five-minute massage.

Markets aren't just a "shopping experience." They are social experiences. Learning experiences. Many of the vendors, like me, spend most of their lives on the farm. We don't get out much. In summer, we work from dawn until dark, and then we're just plumb tuckered out. The market might be the only time we socialize that week. We might see friends at the market in spring for the first time since fall, or bump into someone we haven't seen in years.

As an amateur farmer, I often seek out others who can give me advice or answer my questions. I talk with the honey vendor about beekeeping, discuss organic insect control methods with the gentleman who both practices and teaches on the subject. I seek out the possible reasons my jellies won't jell, discuss the laying habits and egg sizes of different chicken breeds. I gaze wistfully at beautiful jewelry that I can't splurge on unless I sell enough to cover my gas, my table fee, my chicken feed and - even a little of my time.

Likewise, a vendor's table might present a week's worth of work—making and/or harvesting the items, packing and loading the wares there for you to see, and packing up what you don't buy to take it home and pack it for storage or process it so it doesn't go to waste. Some tables include a lifetime's habit of beading for relaxation, a winter's worth of sewing, or eggs that are less than an hour old.

A vendor might have a new product, or a new vendor has come to participate. You might see something you've never seen before, like stuffed animals hand-made from alpaca fur, or a meaty, heirloom tomato that's shaped like a pepper and has very few seeds. The farm-raised beef we got last year was some of the best we'd ever eaten, and I saw lamb available at the market this year. And I can't live without my laundry soap.

I first encountered the Make-Your-Own Laundry Soap Kit four years ago and fell in love. When you live "way-out" as we do, you sure hate to make a trip to town just for laundry soap. But the kit makes ten gallons worth at a time in a five-gallon bucket (which you mix with equal parts water in your laundry bottle that sits by the washer). For the two of us, one kit (ten bucks) lasts about a year. One time, I ran out in winter and had to contact the vendor to mail me a kit.

That beautiful Flowering Quince bush in my front yard? It came to me as a twig in a pot when I won it as a Door Prize at the first local market I ever visited. Likewise, the huge chocolate mint patch in the herb garden (and the jars of jelly in the pantry made from it) all came from a small sprout purchased at a market two years ago.

Even so, a key component at any market is produce. Yet I've noticed, with the availability of products shipped from afar, many people forget that produce is seasonal. Early season markets will have lettuces, peas, radishes, herbs. Local growers with greenhouses or garden tunnels or other cold-weather protectants will have produce "ahead of season" (thank goodness).

Of course, we all love fresh produce. But produce is not the only thing produced by any farm. Produce is not the only point of the Farmer's Market. If you are focusing on the produce, you are missing a large part of the valuables that are there.

Find your local Farmer's Market and go experience it. Lay aside any preconceived notions of what a market is and discover who and what your market is. Who are the regulars? Who's missing? Who can answer your questions? Tell you something new? If you aren't hooked on the first visit, try again later in the season, when your local gardeners and farmers are overwhelmed with produce and come two hours early just to get a market space. Your market is an amazing resource in your community.

Go be a part of it.

Weeding in the Rain, Weeding out the Stuff

"Life isn't about waiting for the storm to pass...It's about learning to dance in the rain." - Vivian Greene

I abandoned our garden for two weeks when I left town to assist my mother who was recuperating from knee replacement surgery. I returned to a forest of weeds. I could still see some of our vegetables (caged tomatoes, tall onion tops gone to seed), but some I had to find again (carrots, hidden blooming pepper plants).

The ground was too wet for the rototiller, so I spent a day making space around the vegetables by weeding by hand. It rained again that evening. The next day I hand-weeded more open space, pulling wet grass and roots out by muddy clumps, still hoping for a full day of sunshine so I could till the next day. But when I looked up, I saw clouds.

By that time, of course, I was hot, sticky, covered in mud from the knees down and elbows out, and had become the main luncheon course for every sweat bee, biting fly and mosquito in the area. But the weeding was not finished. I could see real progress though, and I just kept going, seeing each row as a battle in the ongoing war. I knew I would be bound inside during office hours of the upcoming week, and it was my last opportunity to make great advances. So, when the big, fat raindrops began falling from the sky, I just kept going.

My garden clogs got slippery on the inside so I just kicked them off. When I started slipping in my bare feet, I got down on my knees. While the rain rinsed my face, back, and upper arms, the rest of me was just bathed in mud. But I kept right on weeding because at that point it all felt good. The wetter the ground got, the easier the weeds were to pull. Of course, I found it more difficult to get a good grip on them with wet, muddy hands, but even so, each yank made a bigger impact. Rows emerged again in the jungle. Fruits could be seen popping out on the vines.

When I finished working, I wandered to the porch, caked with mud and dripping as I went. My hair had fallen and stuck to my neck, my fingernails were crammed full of soil and greens. Half red from my weed-eating in the sun and half brown from the mud, I glanced to see the water pouring from the eave spout at the end of the porch, and it only made sense at the time to step into its flow.

There's something about a full day of dirty work that gives you satisfaction and pride as an adult. Likewise, there's something about being covered in mud and standing under the rain spout that appeals to your inner child. At that moment, I had the best of both.

Everyone Needs an Apron

I've recently discovered the usefulness of a 'tool' I have never used before. I don't know if this discovery is a sign of my age or just a symptom of this self-reliant lifestyle I am working to develop. Either way, I must admit, I don't know how I ever managed life without an apron.

Perhaps my years as a waitress in a four-star restaurant confused me about the apron. To this day, I still don't understand why such establishments make their wait staff wear aprons that are white! Of course, in a fancy restaurant, wearing a dirty apron is a cardinal sin, and I always had trouble keeping mine clean. When I left that profession, I could not wait to toss (or burn) that white apron. And I never considered buying, using, or wearing one ever again.

But, a little over a year ago, my mother moved from her large family home into a condo. In the downsizing that ensued, many of her possessions became mine. While some of these effects have marketable value, most were simply items of sentimental value, pieces I could not bear to let go. Two of these 'pieces' were my father's aprons.

I don't recall Mother ever wearing an apron in the kitchen, but I remember my father's shop aprons well. Made of denim, they covered his front from collar bone down, and although I know he must have gotten them dirty, even now they show not a single stain.

I never meant to wear them. I just couldn't let them go. So, I brought them home hoping Frank would perhaps adopt them, saving and preserving some of his clothes. But Frank has "work clothes," shirts and pants he is allowed to get dirty. And so, the aprons hung on the coat rack near the kitchen, untouched for nearly a year.

And then, it came time to string green beans.

Now, it's been almost thirty years since I last spent time stringing beans. Every memory I have of bean stringing is set on the porch of my grandparent's summer cabin Blue, West Virginia, sitting in the porch swing.

I suppose that explains why I felt compelled to head out to our porch swing to tackle the task—a place with no real workspace. With a basket of beans, a bowl for the cleaned beans and a knife, I tried to recall what grandma did with the strings... She dropped them into her lap—a procedure made possible only by the presence of the apron. So, I wandered down the coat rack and put on one of Daddy's.

Immediately, I felt like a professional. Professional gardener, professional cook, professional housewife. My knowledge of cleaning and canning beans came from faded memories and a worn instruction book, but that apron helped me feel like I knew what I was doing. Somehow, putting on the apron made me feel more important, as if I had put on some time-honored uniform.

When I finished stringing the beans, I gathered up the corners of my apron and carried the strings out to the compost pile. Just like grandma did. I began to understand and appreciate the potential usefulness of the apron.

Who needs a basket in the garden? Cucumbers, beans, and peppers fit right into the pockets – as do gardening tools. When the pockets are full, gather the apron corners to make a bag.

While canning, why stop to grab a hand towel to wipe your hands? The apron is there, with you, wherever you are, whatever you are doing. The apron saved my clothes when I pickled eggs in beet juice, and again when I splashed grease from the stove. I thought, "how many shirts could I have saved if I had put on an apron years ago?"

It seems that the popularity of the apron has gone by the wayside along with the simple life. Microwaves, wash and wear clothing, pies from the freezer and not from the oven. Gone are the days when girls learned to make aprons in Home Economics class. Gone are the days when shy toddlers hid behind their mother's apron. Gone are the days when the apron was a staple of the household, a symbol of family dinners and Christmas cookies and noodle dough rolled out in flour on the counter.

When was the last time you saw an apron on sale in the store?

I realize now that it is only natural that I have discovered the use of the apron as I discover and enjoy the pleasures of simple living. I don't know how I ever survived without one.

The Garden Marathon

Feeling the chill of mid-September evenings, I realize now that I have been racing against our garden since mid-July. The summer has come and gone in a flurry of cutting, canning, drying, freezing, packing, cooking, and cleaning up the mess all these things make.

The garden, of course, gets to "tag-team" it. First, we race the beans, then the cucumbers, then the cantaloupe and then, this years' most formidable foe – the tomato patch. For four straight weeks, every possible moment I spent trying to stay ahead of the tomatoes. To be honest, far too many ended up as chicken feed. Even now, banana and sweet peppers and even more tomatoes wait while I take a break from the garden – processing apples from a friends' tree. Never in my life have I processed so much food – nearly all of the things I have never done before.

Although we near the end of the summer growing season, the garden is far from finished. Sweet potatoes, carrots, herbs of all kinds, all still need to be dealt with. It is a lot of work, and getting started was an investment, but nothing store-bought could ever taste so good. Perhaps you are thinking of starting or expanding your garden next year and preserving some food of your own. Let me save you some of the troubles I've had with these few tips:

If you plan on canning large quantities, you'll need more than jars, lids, and a big pot. You'll need a canning funnel, jar tongs, canning salt, sugar by the 25-pound bag, vinegar by the gallons. Purchase a Squeezo. Just do it now. The price is worth the time/effort/energy it saves.

If you are planning to deal with a single hot pepper, buy rubber gloves. And even then, hot pepper burns can be soothed by lemon juice and/or milk.

If you are going to can green beans or meats, buy a pressure canner. Buck up, follow the instructions and be not afraid. (I prefer the kind with the jiggler on top instead of the thermostat.)

Buy an apron. Wear it. Canning is a messy job. You will ruin your clothes.

Always purchase wide-mouth jars. Not all things work well in small-mouth jars (pickled eggs, hot pepper hot dogs), but everything works in a wide-mouth jar. Three years from now when you've amassed a collection of jars and rings and of different sizes and portions, you'll be glad they're interchangeable.

If there are only two people in your home, purchase more pints than quarts. A quart is usually too much for two people in one meal.

When designing pantry storage, plan space for both full jars and empty ones. If you have filled your storage space canned goods, where will you store the jars as you empty them?

Before you put a single saucepot or canning pot on your stove, cover the whole stovetop in aluminum foil, and cut out holes for the burners. (Unless, of course, you want to spend hours scrubbing your stovetop when you are finished with all the canning.)

Leave picked produce outside of the house until you are ready to deal with it. Two words: Fruit flies.

Don't peel pumpkins. You will be there all day. Instead, slice them in half, de-seed, and put them cut-side down in a pan of water in the oven a 350 for about 15-20 minutes. Then, cool a little and scoop the pulp out of the shell.

Don't make catsup or apple butter on the stove unless you want to stand there stirring, heating up the house, all day. Put the whole pot in the oven on low and bake it overnight. Make applesauce in the crockpot while the apple butter's in the oven.

When making jelly, add a pat of butter to fruit before adding sugar and pectin. It will make it easier to keep that required, one-minute, rolling boil without the pot bubbling over and getting sticky stuff everywhere. If it still doesn't gel, label it "syrup" and use it on ice cream, cakes or as a marinade.

To keep from crying when you cut a large quantity of onions for salsas, sauces or soups, place the onions in the freezer for five minutes before you deal with them.

Label every jar lid with the contents inside and the year canned. Properly canned goods will keep more than a year. You don't want to get them confused with next year's goods.

Don't toss the boxes the jars come in. They are the easiest way to store the empty jars so they don't get broken. Put them upside down in the box to keep the dust from getting inside. With the boxes, you'll also have an idea how much space you'll need to have all the empties in one place -- ready to go when you need them next year.

I have lots of recipe books, but few of them included these helpful hints - many that I had to learn the hard way. After three years now of gardening and canning, this has been our most ambitious yet, and we were fortunate to have more experienced folks around us to help us overcome some of our challenges. Some things we had to figure out on our own.

This year's canning season was a marathon, and I don't know if we won or if the garden did. But at least we're going to finish the race with over 200 jars in the pantry and 100 bags in the freezers. I'm sure, next year's race we'll do even better, and I'll keep this list of tips to help me get a head start. But right now, I'm awfully tired.

SIMPLE LIFE

The Importance of Practicality

Not long after completing my undergraduate degree, I spent a year living in a secluded house on a ridge point, surrounded by the forests of Wirt County. Bath and wash water came from the rain on the roof, funneled by the gutters into a basement cistern. Heat for summer cooking came from a hot plate or grill, and heat for the house in winter came from the woodstove.

Viable work was in Parkersburg, over an hour away. But there a recent sawmill site over the next hill offered plenty of firewood, and I tutored students for income. I could pay my electric, rent, and groceries. Water from the cistern and heat from the mill leftovers were both free.

Once a month, I traveled to town for food and to do laundry, and for the remainder of the year, I stayed in that house on the hill, for I could afford little else. That year includes some of the most profound, the most relaxed, the most enlightening moments of my life.

Splitting and carrying wood and water when needed is hard labor, and it was hard living, especially for a city girl. But at the end of the day, I would sit, dead tired on the back porch, and watch the sun set from my perch on top of the mountain.

Once settled into the house, my daily routine began to include creative writing (with pen and paper), gardening, carrying water and wood, walking the dogs, and watching the sunset. In other words, my adult life had never before--or has ever since--been more simple.

It is incredibly difficult to live so simply in this world and the limited period when I was able to do so (and survive it) now seems to be nothing but a fleeting collection of memories of when my only purpose each day was of my own choosing. Time flowed fluid but thick like molasses and slow as ketchup. I told time by the position of the sun in the sky, by the passing of the school busses on the roads far below me. On top of a solitary mountain, the night sky surrounds you, and the rest of the world just fades away...

Then a job opportunity came, and I gladly and thankfully took it. I became a functioning citizen of the world again and at the time, was happy to do so. But now, some years later, I think back on those days when I tended gardens in the morning, wrote stories and taught in the heat of the day, carried wood and walked dogs in the evenings, and closed each day with the sunset.

Our lives in this modern world are so complicated. It is as though we are trained and drained by the mechanisms that are meant to make our lives easier. While I may sit and wish I could go back to that mountain, I know that the way for me to get back to that frame of mind (what I'm truly longing for) is to give up the items I don't truly need in life and simplify.

We're all being squeezed by economic conditions; we're all running in a reactive mode simply answering the demands for our attention. We're all scrambling, in one way or another, to regain some sense of peace, of control, to get to a point where we are "at rest." But if our lives are complicated, how can we ever be at rest?

Since my husband and I left the house on the mountain, we've worked to be that settled again, that organized again, that "simplified" again. In all these years, we still haven't accomplished it. These days, I "need" my cell phone. I "need" my computer and my Internet, and my make-up and my specialty teas and flavored creamer. Alas, thirteen years of modern living has ruined me. My life is no longer simple.

Since I can no longer master the simple life, I have chosen a different goal--a practical life. I've been working to become a more practical person. This approach is helping purge our home of unnecessary items we have become slaves to. Cleaning out closets and storage and kitchen drawers becomes much easier when you ask: "Is it useful?" and "Is it worth the time/expense needed to take care of it?"

While all this might seem too basic to improve our lives, we have found that as we "purge" out the unnecessaries of our lives, we slowly but surely, begin to relax more, and have a greater appreciation for the items we've chosen to keep. We have the time to take care of what we have, and more time to take care of ourselves and each other.

A simple life is a practical life, and it is obviously practical to work towards a life that isn't burdened by unnecessary possessions. In a culture where we are typically defined by what we have and what we live with, I have learned that often, it is easier to live without.

Cards, Board Games, and Spoons

We're huddled inside around the gas stove. Dandelion, our yellow tabby (who was supposed to be an outside cat), lays sprawled on the floor in front of the stove. Daisy, our beagle-child, lies next to me in the nearby overstuffed writing chair. Frank is at the worktable behind the stove, studying the lenses for his new camera.

We've been huddled in like this for three days now, only venturing out for chickens, chores, and trips to the mailbox.

It seems natural to hibernate like this, to curl up around a warm fire and work on quiet, introspective projects. I imagine farmers huddled with seed catalogs and planning their gardens, grandmothers crocheting scarves and slippers at warm kitchen tables. Family members taking turns adding wood to the home fires.

When I was young, days like these (when it is far too cold to be outside for long), we played cards and board games. Monopoly, Clue, Trivial Pursuit, Chinese Checkers, Checkers, Scrabble, Boggle, UNO, Hearts, and Rummy. My father liked to play chess, but I was never good at it. My sister played much better than I, willing to exert the effort to remember what cards had been played in previous hands.

I've always looked at games as something where it doesn't matter if you win or lose. It's a game. It only matters that you play. I always like UNO and Clue, even though my mother won Clue more often than not. A more recent favorite is Apples to Apples, where even the winner is disappointed when the game comes to an end because the fun is in the play, not the win. Board games aren't as popular these days. Families hardly gather around a table for dinner together, much less for playtime. I wonder how many Scrabble boards are gathering dust in the closet while their owners play Words with Friends online. How many video game thumbs have slipped up a ladder or swooped down a chute? How many social skills are developed by yelling Sorry or You sank my battleship? I wonder, how much stress is relieved by screaming Yahtzee?

Board and card games are for everyone to play. No one needs to have mastered a hand-held controller, no one needs to have a college degree.

Board games and card games are some of my fondest memories. We would have popcorn and finger foods and Kool-Aid with the radio playing Top 40's and weather reports. I don't remember any specific game losses or wins; I don't recall any poignant conversations over cards. But I remember how my father rolled the dice in his large, callused hands, how my mother meticulously fanned the cards in her hands, how my sister taught me to shuffle. And I remember laughter.

Wins and losses, I forget. But I remember the family around the table, plastic seasonal tablecloths and wearing the Monopoly top hat on my little finger. I remember sweating glasses of sun tea, the names of all the culprits in Clue, how hard it is for me to get a blue pie piece in Trivial Pursuit, the sound of the Pop-O-Matic die roller in the game of Trouble. I used to thrive on examining other people's shuffle and dealing styles.

I hate to think this kind of fun is going by the wayside. Even snowed in, Frank and I have been known to break out the Reversi board, or to thumb through random Trivial Pursuit cards. Why not revive a nonvideo game in your household? Pick one of your old favorites or try this old favorite of mine. Spoons can be played by anyone of any age, requires little to no strategy, and always brings about humorous results.

HOW TO PLAY SPOONS: The game requires: a standard deck of cards (no Jokers) and Spoons, one fewer than there are players. Three to 13 people can play.

Arrange the spoons in a small circle in the center of the table and deal four cards to each player. Each player tries to make four of a kind.

The dealer takes a card off the top of the deck to have five cards in his hand, removes one and passes it facedown to the left. Each player discards to the person on his left.

The last player places his discard into a trash pile. Cards are picked up and passed quickly around the table until someone gets four of a kind and takes a spoon from the center.

Once the player with four of a kind takes a spoon, anyone can take a spoon. The player left without a spoon gets a letter from the word Spoon.

The player who reaches four of a kind can do a "sneaky pull" of a spoon, exposing those paying too close attention to their cards. An obvious grab can lead to a wild free-for-all.

(If at any time the draw cards run out, pause to reshuffle the trash pile and keep going.)

Players move closer to elimination each time they don't get a spoon and take the next letter in the word S-P-O-O-N. Spell it and you are out. The winner is the last player remaining.

The Stuff of Life

When Frank and I got together, he had bachelor stuff and I had bachelorette stuff. Together, that gave us a house with "his and hers" stuff. When we moved back to the farm, settled with more space, we began to get "our" stuff, like "our" couch, "our" television. We also started getting "hand-me-down" stuff from friends and family – things they didn't need anymore that we might need someday.

So then, we had more and more stuff.

Then I had an auction, yard sale and thrift store phase. More stuff.

Then, in the middle of winter, my mother moved from a 3-bedroom, 2-story house with a full attic to a condo. In the process of getting her stuff condensed and moved, we had a huge influx of all kinds of stuff here at home – sentimental stuff, family history stuff, antique stuff, valuable stuff, collections of stuff, general stuff, and to-be-sorted stuff.

We became over-stuffed.

Now slaves to our stuff, we made a pact: we were going to get rid of stuff.

We had a yard sale, which helped get rid of we'll never use it stuff, never liked it in the first place stuff, and why do we even have this stuff. But, it also created a new series of stuff, the "didn't sell at the yard sale" stuff.

We began recycling. Then we had sorted piles of stuff to be recycled – at different locations. Yes, the piles occasionally were carted away, only for new piles to begin.

None of this worked well. We were sorting and moving stuff around, but not enough stuff actually left our domain.

So, we adopted The Pass or Trash Mindset. The Pass and Trash mindset is two-fold: if we can't use it, pass it to someone who can, and, if no one can, trash it. This beefed up the Recycling approach and helped me get rid of sweeper bags that fit sweepers I no longer have, a Sony Playstation we never play, coats we never wear. It also adheres to the concept that if it is broken, torn, stained or otherwise needing repair or mending that will never happen – trash it. The Pass and Trash mindset is incredibly helpful with clothes.

Then, we took on The Can It Be Made Use Of Mindset. Most people refer to this as "Reusing," and it also kept the Recycling approach rolling. This is the thought process that results in a glass hanging lamp globe serving as a garden ball. This is how an old console television cabinet now stores postal supplies. This is how old refrigerator baskets end up storing potatoes and onions, and how coffee pots with holes burned through the bottom become homes for potted plants.

By this time, I had collected a lot of stuff I wanted to keep but didn't know what to do with. I began The Serious, Organized Storage Mindset. If I wouldn't need it often, store it safely and properly. Blankets, pillows, and craft supplies were placed in plastic bins. Family heirlooms were wrapped and put in wooden trunks with cedar balls. If I needed it regularly, I made some kind of storage system for it. Pictures were sorted and placed into albums, books, CD's and movies were sorted, purged and arranged in proper order. Cords were rolled and placed in popcorn tins, magazines were chronologically collected into magazine boxes.

At this point, I began to see a light at the end of the tunnel. We began to see Empty Space. Empty spaces allow your mind to breathe and require no maintenance or dusting. The more Empty Space I began to see, the more I liked it.

And that's when I began The Do I Love It Enough to Deal With It Mindset. We live in the country. I have to dust at least once a week. And as I continued through this weekly chore, I realized – I would be dusting this stuff every week for the rest of my life. Knick knacks, memorabilia, nostalgic burdens – all on display waiting for that weekly dust off. I began to realize – many of them I did not love that much. Goodbye to the gnome figurine gifted from a high school boyfriend. Goodbye to a collection of rocks from different hiking trips. Goodbye to candlesticks that don't match, vases that haven't held flowers in fifteen years. Goodbye old phone books and bent out of shape baskets.

In addition, I began to value storage space more than some stuff. In order to deal with some stuff, I had to store it, using space in high demand. I began to realize, I was no longer willing to store this stuff. Goodbye to several kitchen appliances. Goodbye to all holiday decorations not related to Christmas. Goodbye to things I may, or may not, use someday.

It has taken four years to get from "having way too much stuff" to "having an almost manageable amount of stuff." But, I find I am now drawn to the scattered empty spaces that are appearing in our lives. Physical empty spaces, and empty spaces of time no longer spent moving, sorting, maintaining, cleaning, rearranging, seeking, losing or otherwise dealing with so much stuff.

We still have way too much stuff. But I'm happy to dust my Grandmother's Bell collection, and the three-foot-tall ceramic owl my mother painted when I was a child. I'm comfortable knowing my father's Navy memorabilia, my grandmother's quilts and two generations of family home movies are stored properly for safe-keeping. I find my stack of labeled plastic bins aesthetically pleasing. And, with these new mindsets, I'm getting rid of more and more stuff every day.

Because the more stuff we get rid of, the more we appreciate the stuff we keep.

Looking into the Past to Prepare for the Future

Several years ago, for a short time, Frank and I lived in the house my grandfather was born in. Only one of his siblings remained, but she had fallen and broken her hip and moved in with her daughter. The house remained just as she left it.

Alone, at her age, she had not been able to maintain the house and farm as she once had. Frank and I, living there, began to clean, clear, and organize.

In sorting through the spare bedroom (which had become a storage room of sorts) I found an entire box of elastic bands cut from little boys' underwear. In another box, I found a collection of dry-rotted thread pieces.

At first, I was confused. Then, I remembered. Elvie, my Great Aunt, had survived The Great Depression.

I thought more about the "clutter" there on the farm. Cider jugs and pickling crocks in the pump house, empty canning jars in the cellar house with boxes of little plate-glass lids for them, a wringer washer on the back porch and clothesline nearby.

At the time, these things were foreign to me. I had never had my own garden, never harvested my own food. Never as an adult had I hung my clothes on the line. I had never, actually, pinched a penny.

At the time, I saw those jars as clutter. Boy, I wish I had them now.

As a publisher, I spend much of my time learning to be ready for the future. What's new in publishing, current trends, about current and future technologies. Most of this I can learn through the Internet.

But as a country girl living on a farm in trying economic times, to be ready for the future, it seems I need to be learning things of the past. Many times I've closed my eyes to pull up a childhood memory of my Grandmother canning green beans to see if I could recall the details of her method. Many times I've contemplated the fact that my Grandfather never had a fence around his garden.

Many times I've wished I had them in the room with me to remind me how they did it. Sure, I can read books or online articles to learn, but believe me – it is not the same as having someone to teach you – especially when you follow the written instructions, and they didn't work...

Our attempts at self-reliance, saving money, gardening, canning and making from scratch are all trial and error. We have yet to grow a decent crop of corn or potatoes, and although I've managed canning and freezing well enough, my first attempts at dry root storage were not completely successful.

Our system for recycling couldn't handle our habits for waste (I never realized I drank so much milk) and resulted in multiple piles of plastic, aluminum, magazines, and cardboard – stashed beneath the porch stairs outside.

After two years, I still can't get every loaf of bread to rise right. About every sixth or seventh loaf rises, then falls – flat. Half of my recipe books call for ingredients (white wine, yellow cake mix) that I no longer keep around the house on a regular basis. I lost four trays of tomato seedlings to dampening, and in my mind, I picture empty spaces on the pantry shelf where spaghetti sauce should be.

Today, Americans are struggling to learn to live better with less, when only two generations before mine, it was a way of life. Canning jars that have been empty and gathering dust in cellar houses and barns are being washed and checked for chips around the rims. Clotheslines are appearing in yards across the country.

But our mindset (and the problems with our economy) has not fully changed. A clothesline and some home canned goods are not enough to "survive" a depression. Apparently, it also takes boxes of elastic waistbands and short little pieces of thread.

When you think "salad," do you think of back yard dandelion greens and nasturtium blossoms and nettle? No, and even if you did think of it, would you know how to fix that salad? I may have chickens in my back yard, but I have no intention of eating them, nor would I have any clue as to how to deal with the feathers.

These days, I sometimes think it might be a good idea to learn.

I feel fortunate to live where there are people around me who well know these skills of self-reliance. People who were my age before they ever ate green beans from a can, or ever heard of a microwave. Our family, our neighbors, friends – they are all more than happy to teach us how to "do for ourselves" when we ask for help. I've noticed an increase in classes and workshops about these topics in our region as well.

Learning the skills from others will get us a long way on our path to saving and making the most of what we've got, but it only takes us halfway. We can learn the theory and the concepts, but we have to practice and change our overall way of thinking and behaving. We can learn how to do, but we also have to learn to undo. We have to undo wasteful habits that are now built into our culture. We need to change our mindset.

I've recently begun using energy formerly spent on worry on making that change instead.

When I worry or talk about energy costs, I look around and see how many lights are on around me. I look to see how many electrical devices are using electricity, even if they are turned off. I realize I'm paying that clock on the DVD player to flash at me.

When I worry about food prices, I look in our refrigerator. How many leftovers are in there going to waste that could be frozen and later used in a casserole or stew? How many plants in our yard can I identify as edible? How many do we use on a regular basis in our salad or meals? We live in a region where food grows wild if we have the mindset to recognize and use it as such.

When I worry about gas prices, I think how often I drive when I can walk. How often I ride alone when I could ride with someone else. No more do we run to town for a single purpose or item, and more often we check with local family and friends to see if they need anything, since we're going.

We worry and we go through the motions, but have we truly changed? By putting my worries into changing my actions and behavior, I feel a little more in control. I lose some of that sense of worry.

This is no Great Depression. We're just feeling the squeeze. The Great Depression was so great that years after it passed, the people who experienced it still saved boxes of elastic waistbands from their underwear! Did Aunt Elvie let the water run while brushing her teeth or leave lights on all over the house? No. Likely never.

People who survived the Great Depression knew how to make a salad without ever going to the store. They knew how to make remedies and brooms, pickles and bread. They made quilts and patched clothes by lamplight or gas lights, and they knew how to make use of everything they had.

Even elastic waistbands and pieces of thread.

Simple Living's Greatest Challenge? Being Still

"To know what counts and what doesn't, you have to know what you are dedicating your life to." Richard Templar, The Rules of Life

When you plan to simplify your life, you begin whittling away the extra-curriculars. Everything you have requires maintenance and upkeep. In order to simplify you must dispose of the possessions that aren't important, aren't necessary. You begin to focus on the remaining items, deciding which are priorities and which are not.

As you dispose of the unnecessaries, you begin to discover time. Imagine the hours of time you spend watching television; looking for tools in an unorganized garage; dusting trinkets throughout the house; keeping up and maintaining objects you don't love or need or even use. Imagine, what you would do with that time.

When we are busy and wrapped up in the world, all the messages and expectations of the world layer themselves over the true thoughts and feelings of our own. We don't understand sometimes why we behave as we do, why we crave what we don't need, why we spend time on obsessions that aren't important.

How often do we wish for more time? Time to think, time to relax, time to rest. But the truth is, we don't know what to do with the time when we have it. We fill our time with busyness, because we have no idea, and no real desire, to be still.

So many of the unnecessary fads in our lives we must maintain our image. So much of our lives is spent maintaining fascinations we identify ourselves with - features we think we need to "survive" in this world, "compete" in this world. Part of simplifying life is peeling away these layers of crazes that truly have no practical use. Things you bought and never wore, used once, broke and never fixed, gadgets you thought you "had to have" when truly, you didn't.

Rediscovering yourself and releasing yourself from these unnecessary burdens in life can be liberating. It can also be - disturbing. Because the input of our hearts and souls has been buried so long, we don't even know what compels us, what we truly need, what is truly important. In order to live a meaningful, mindful life, you must listen to your mind and discover what gives your life meaning.

When you have stripped away the items the marketers have told us we need to survive, you are left with yourself -- exactly as you are. Wow. After years of listening to the world and spending our time on contraptions that don't nourish us? What's left of us when our consumer skin is torn away -- well, it ain't pretty.

One of the benefits and keys of simple living is learning to work with what you've got. In order to do that, you must assess what's there, assess the potential, and find the right use for it. I have old wire shelving in the garden for peas to climb. I have former refrigerator baskets in the chicken pen for nesting boxes. I have a broken patio umbrella in the chicken yard to give the ladies daily shade, and I'm working with a flawed, middle-aged human self who has recently discovered a desire to live the simple life, with little experience but the ability to learn and willingness to try.

You can't know what truly counts in your life and what doesn't unless you know what is important to you. There's a big chance that the voice that tells you what is important is not your own. When I cleared away all the voices that were telling me what was important in my life, I was left with -- questions.

Learning to raise hens, plant and harvest a garden, bake your own bread -- these are relatively easy. Rediscovering who you are, deciding what is truly important, redefining your goals and dealing with all these adjustments? Not so easy. But it's a side effect of simplifying your life. When you have created the time to just be, you must face yourself.

Being still means facing this person that is you, the person beneath the cars, clothing, technology. When you are still, you must discover and assess the person you are when you are stripped of the world's demands and expectations.

Ever have a city mouse visit you in the country? Quite often, they can't sit still. They've come away to relax, but sittin' on the porch swing watchin' the grass grow reveals the ants in their pants. As soon as possible, they want to go somewhere, do something -- anything. When given the chance to truly relax, they just don't know how.

We can't blame them. I know exactly how they feel. Learning to be still - it takes practice if you've been busy all your life. Learning to be still also takes courage, because you are left with the rambling thoughts and worries of your own mind. A mind that's been trained to need, want, have, achieve more. Being still requires contentment, an ease with the current conditions of your life and yourself. If you've spent years looking and wanting for more, more, more - being still takes some getting used to.

Over time, I've come to face the me that's left, accepting that "this is what I've got to work with." Now I'm seeking the answers for what to do with it. I still working to learn to sit still. But this is sitting still, not being still. The only place where I have found it possible so far to be still is in the porch swing—and I plan to get in a lot of practice there this season.

The Economy of a Community

I was 21 years old when I moved out of my parent's house and into my first apartment. I served as a waitress at a four-star restaurant, so I cooked little, and my income was mostly cash. The kitchen canisters I bought when I furnished the new place were never filled with flour, sugar, coffee or tea, so to budget myself, I re-labeled them: Rent, Electric, Water, Phone. Next to the canisters stood a jar for change.

When I got home from work each night and emptied my cash earnings from my pockets, I separated the bills into the canisters - bigger bills in "Rent" and "Electric," smaller bills in "Water" and "Phone." I put cash in my wallet for groceries and gas, and any leftover change went into the jar.

Not the most advanced accounting system, I admit. Years passed before I seriously learned about budgeting and money management, and I do not imply that I have perfected either. But when you begin your independent life as a "responsible" adult rolling change at the end of every month to pay your bills, and you learn early on that $25 is three or four good tables you have to serve, on your feet, carrying heavy trays and trying not to get your white apron dirty... You quickly become what I call an "alternative shopper."

Yard sales, thrift shops, outlet stores, flea markets. When you are 21 and your savings consists of a bag full of rolled quarters, and you want a coffee table, you don't go to the furniture store. You go to Goodwill or the Salvation Army Store, then you go to the discount store for a cheap can of paint.

You would think though, later in life, as I graduated college, entered "the real world," and got paychecks and bank accounts and better budgeting skills, I would go to the furniture store for a coffee table. But alas, my outlook has already been skewed. I may purchase my couch, my bed, and other "big purchase" items at a regular retail store, sure, but when I look at a shiny new, $400 coffee table, I know, somewhere out there, there's a great table for 25 bucks that just needs a good coat of paint or stain.

I would love to have a shiny, new coffee table. What I have is a yard sale find with two shelves, and when I bought it, water-stained with one loose leg. Cost? Ten bucks. I removed the legs, (making the bottom shelf the bottom of the table), added rollers on the bottom, and upholstered the top with a piece of padded, baby blue vinyl I found at another yard sale for five bucks.

No, it's not shiny and new, but I can roll it out of the way when I'm vacuuming, and I can set a glass of iced tea on it without using a coaster. Yeah, I'm big on alternative shopping.

In my community, it seems there is a constant exchange of canned goods, produce, labor, clothes. Articles worn by the last newborn (now a toddler), can be seen on a recent newborn, whom everyone wants to hold. One person has apples, another has eggs, another has the tool needed to do the neighbor's job, but not the tool to do his own. It seems we have our own little economy here, based on trade and barter and exchange of services.

I'm comforted to be living in the central West Virginia hills—especially during harvest and deer season--when more and more Americans struggle to stretch their dollars. It seems here, in so many ways, the dollar isn't the only tool we have for survival. Sure, we need dollars to fill those 'canisters' to pay our bills, but in many other ways, we only have to share our need with others, and the solution comes from some unpredicted place.

When I sit down to a meal of venison smothered in shiitake mushrooms, with applesauce, and green beans--and realize there isn't an item being served that I actually paid for with money (whether I harvested it myself or not) I feel compelled to be thankful. But it happens so regularly here, some folks don't even give it a second thought.

The Price of a Penny

Every year, the United States goes $900 million more in debt from making money. That's right. Each year, our national debt rises that much alone from making pennies and nickels. You see, it costs 1.5 cents to make a penny, and seven cents to make a nickel. We've all heard the saying, "it takes money to make money," and yet, in this case, a penny made is not a penny earned. For every dollar's worth of pennies we make, we're losing 50 cents. For every dollar's worth of nickels, we lose 40 cents.

To you and me, the solution for this is a "no-brainer." Use a cheaper metal to make these coins. It's been done before.

The U.S. penny since 1982 is made of 99.2% zinc and 0.8% copper, with the outside plated with copper. Before 1982 pennies were made of solid copper, all except in 1943 when pennies were made of steel plated with zinc because copper was in short supply due to WWII.

So we changed the penny when we didn't have the copper, can't we change the cost to make a penny now when we can't afford the growing debt?

It may seem simple to you and me, but today's policy-makers and decision-makers will be quick to say, "It isn't that simple." In fact, for more than a decade, the "what to do with the penny" argument has continued, with no agreement reached, costing us more than $9000 million dollars alone from minting pennies while waiting for a decision.

Some will argue that it would be better to just do away with the penny. Oh, I see, so you can round everything up to the nearest five. But then, it costs too much to make a nickel so then we should round up to the nearest ten – on taxes? Percentages? Now THAT seems complicated to me.

Others would argue that changing the composition would affect the copper or zinc industry, resulting in a huge loss of jobs, resulting in an increase of those on assistance, which would, in the long term, create more debt than printing pennies.

Even others would note that our money, in reality, has no value anyway. And they too would be right. Since 1933, when President Roosevelt outlawed private ownership of gold (except for jewelry) and took our monetary system off of The Gold Standard (when the value of money was based on the price of gold). Our money became valueless. In fact, nearly all monetary systems in the world today are based on the Fiat System where (and I quote) "money that is intrinsically useless; is used only as a medium of exchange."

So, how does it feel to know that since 1971, when the last major world money system switched over, that the world's money has been useless?

Today, when a dollar (or even a hundred dollars) seems to go nowhere, while policymakers discuss the condition of our "worthless" economy, perhaps it is time for us country folk to turn to another system that we've been using for years – The Barter System.

Bartering is a medium in which goods or services are directly exchanged for other goods and/or services, without the use of money. Folks around here call it horse tradin'. Barter usually replaces money as the method of exchange in times of monetary crisis, when the currency is unstable and devalued. In fact, these days, the worldwide organized barter exchange and trade industry has grown to an $8 billion a year industry and is used by thousands of businesses and individuals.

Up to 70% of the economy in rural communities through the world is through the barter system. In fact, some economists would say that the barter system has contributed to the downfall of our rural communities, and if we were to pay for the goods and services we require, instead of using the barter system, it would boost our local economy, and provide services for the community.

In other words, our exchange system prevents us from reaching successful levels of participation in their exchange system.

But gee, it seems to me that their system is broken, and our barter system is going to flourish.

Personally, I like the barter system. In the barter system, the only person who can tell you the value of your tomato is the person you are trying to trade with. A tomato isn't worth $2.49. It might be worth an apple, or two apples, or an egg.

In the nation's economy, there are those who have and those who don't. And what we have is worth less every day. Every dollar saved only gets us 50 cents ahead. But, in the horse tradin' business, we all have something of value. Vegetables, skills, products, services, car parts, animals, all have varying levels of value – directly depending on the other person's needs.

Remember those 1943 pennies? The ones made of steel to save copper in our country's crisis of World War II? Because of a simple mistake, in the changeover from 1942's contents to 1943's contents, an unknown number of 1943 pennies were created with a mixture of both, creating the penny collector's "golden calf", the copper-alloy cent. Coin experts speculate that they were struck by accident when copper-alloy 1-cent blanks remained in the press hopper when production began on the new steel pennies. The mistake happened at all three mints in the country – Philadelphia, Denver, and San Francisco.

There are fewer than 40 copper-alloy cents assumed to be left in existence today. But if you find one, a feel like trading it, what is its true monetary value?

It could be worth up to $82,000 dollars – but only if you find the right person to trade. But you can't eat a penny, you can't drive it. You can't heat with it, take shelter in it, and it will not grow and produce. And if the coin collector invested his money in the stock market, he may no longer have that $82,000 to offer you. So then it's actually not even worth a single cent.

While the world tries to figure out the value of a dollar, I think we should all consider the value of a trade. Trading isn't an "under the table" exchange any more. It is a growing, respected industry based on an exchange system that will only become more and more popular over the next several years. Businesses can legally account for trades for the IRS by assigning a monetary value to the items or service exchanged and reporting it along with all other expenses and incomes.

These days, when everyone is thinking about money, money is barely worth talking about. If you are feeling low about your current "financial worth," put on your tradin' hat and take another inventory of your assets. You may discover you have great worth after all.

Dependencies

Water. I'm confident many West Virginians have a different concept of water today than they did before The Elk River chemical spill (when crude 4-methylcyclohexanemethanol (MCHM) was released into the Elk River and to 300,000 residents were without access to potable water.) We are so accustomed to safe, clear, running water that we don't give water a second thought. However, a derecho storm or a chemical spill can force us to face how dependent we are on water.

When we lived on the ridge in Wirt County, we lived without city water or even a well. We had an indoor outhouse that required no water, and we collected the rainwater from our roof for washing and showering. The gutters on the house ran into a 50-gallon drum my father set up, filled with layers of stone and screen. Smaller rock and smaller weave screens were near the bottom, larger rocks and larger screens near the top where the gutters flowed in. A pipe coming out the bottom of the barrel fed into a cistern in the basement.

Although we didn't drink the rainwater ourselves, we used it to water the animals, to cook with, to bathe and wash with. And the water we collected in a year would last us a year - - almost. Late August was always a low water time. Just when it seemed we needed it most.

There are many ways to "leave the grid" and become more self-sustainable. But none of us can live without water. For any living situation, it is a primary, essential concern. Plants, pets, family - without clean water, we all perish.

This recent water disaster (nicknamed the "Aquapocalypse") could be - and should be - a wake-up call. We should all be examining who we trust to provide for us, to look out for our best interests, and how little respect we have as Americans for the true necessities of life.

I've come to realize that I will watch the decline of our environment and planet for the rest of my life. I have listened to scientists who have spent their entire careers speaking for the environment. Now aged and in their retirement, they wonder if their life's work has made any difference at all. How terribly discouraged they must feel. They and others believe that many will be challenged to have the basic necessities of life in the future.

I grew up watching M*A*S*H, a sit-com based at a mobile medical unit during the Korean War. The story was pertinent to us since my father was a medic in the Korean War. In one episode, Hawkeye, one of the main characters, is called to a Korean home to tend to an aging woman. In the ensuing conversation, he discovers that the family's water source was a mile from the home. "You walk a mile every day for water?" He asked the woman's daughter. "That's where the water is," she replied.

Before my father set up the filtering system for our water on that hill in Wirt County, we carried water. We gathered, bottled, purchased it where we could, and carried it. In the winter and spring, when we had to park at the top of the driveway, we carried it about half a mile. Water is heavy, and water is life. Humans can last for days without food, but not without water. When you must carry every drop of water you need more than half a mile, you build a relationship to it. You begin to take extra efforts not to waste a single drop.

As Americans, we use approximately 408 billion gallons of water a DAY. In 1950, about 62% of the population was dependent on public water systems. By the year 2000, 85% of the population was dependent on public water. These days, with public water systems being privatized, more than 95% of the American population gets water from a commercial enterprise of one kind or another. More than 95% of the population is dependent on someone else for their water, one of life's main necessities.

A similar percentage of Americans are dependent on someone else for their supply of food as well. Think on that a minute. We are a nation dependent on government systems and corporations for our food, energy, and water. Entities that require money for exchange who, it often seems, are out to destroy our planet. That's just scary. How dependent are you? Support safety and environmental regulations. Our necessities of life might depend on it.

Consider Self-Reliance

When I look back on the year (2012), it would be easy to focus on the negatives. Terms like tragedy, superstorm, hurricane, derecho, explosions - even massacre come to mind. Here in our relatively secluded home environment where we live without the constant barrage of mainstream media, we cannot escape the spew of bad news.

It can't be a secret that Frank and I have a little "prepper" in us. Obviously, I don't believe the Mayan Calendar theory or other doomsday theories of the end of the world--or I wouldn't be writing this. But when you try to live your lives as your grandparents did - raising your own food, becoming more self-sufficient, learning to manage and protect your own - it is part of the process to prepare for a bad season.

Our grandparents put up more canned goods, bales, food than they needed to because there might just not be any next year. Saving for a rainy day wasn't just a saying, it was a cultural reality. There was no guarantee the crops would do well the next year, no assurances that the coming winter would be as mild as the one before. The "old-timers" always put up extra wood, extra hay, extra food - if/when they had it.

In perspective, it is amazing that in two generations, we've become a society that expects it all to be guaranteed. We expect the lights to come on when we flip a switch, the water to pour when we turn the spigot. We expect the store shelves to be stocked, to have health care provided, to have our government supervise and regulate our food supply in our best interest. We expect, we expect, we expect - comfort, convenience, and even our health and security - all to be provided for us without fail. Why are we be surprised when we are disappointed or experience discomfort or even drastic losses? Why do we expect someone else to care for our needs?

Consider the concept of self-reliance. What some people call "prepping," we call common sense and logic. Prepping has recently again become a trend in our country, yet many don't realize that there are principles behind the concept. Here's a brief overview of the five principles of preparedness from americanpreppersnetwork.com.

1. Be Thrifty and Frugal - The depression-era saying of "Use it up, wear it out, make it do, or do without" covers this concept. Living thriftily is a simple, effective, and immediate method to increase your spending power.

2. Seek Independence - Live independent of the entrapping influences of society as much as possible. Free your mind of thinking you need a better-looking car, a prettier house, or better clothes. Not only seek to become independent from debt, but also of the influences of; caffeine, alcohol, drugs, tobacco, unhealthy food, medications (where possible) and so on. All these things not only make you a personal slave to addictions but also indenture your wallet to spending wasteful amounts of money.

3. Be Industrious - Learn, Explore, Do. Manage your circumstance to your advantage, be enterprising, and fully explore opportunities that come your way. Become a lifelong learner and constantly work to develop new skills. Being industrious means getting up and attempting something – even if it has the potential to fail. Your successes have the potential to be life-changing.

4. Strive to be Self Reliant - Self-reliance is predicated by - and builds upon - the first three principles. They are unavoidably intertwined and interdependent. Self-Reliance is, in its simplest form, being able to create or provide all needed things as the result of labor, and being able to provide resources as a result of judiciously storing needful things. Self-Reliance is the process of developing skills and talents while putting away resources. When combined with thrift and frugality, self-reliance is providing needed things for yourself that would otherwise cost you money. When combined with independence, self-reliance drives us to be truly reliant on ourselves in all areas. Self-Reliance is the act of being free of needing others, including companies, the government, or your community to provide for or support you. It requires research, learning, experimenting, failing, experimenting more and finally succeeding - being industrious.

5. Aspire to Have Supplies - The natural outgrowth of self-reliance is the storage of things that are essential for our family's ensured safety, comfort, and existence. This includes food, clothing, water, heat, power, home medical supplies, fire starters, light, and so on. Most preppers have a goal to amass a year's supply of their needs. This may seem extreme for some, but how many went 10-14 days without electricity this summer after the derecho storm? How long before relief and aid arrived in the New York region after Hurricane Sandy? In Louisiana after Hurricane Katrina? In West Virginia after the devastating floods? At least set a goal to have a month's supply on hand, so you can also help your neighbors if needed.

You don't have to believe in doomsday theories to be prepared for emergencies. The lessons we learned this year (and in years since) have given us an opportunity to witness, grow, and become more responsible for our own safety and security. And while it seemed this year was fraught with challenges and disasters; the silver lining of those clouds is that we can make sure we are ready - when such disasters strike again. There's no reason to be afraid, but there is reason to be prepared.

Pick one or two of these principles to enact in your life. You may be surprised to find, as I did, that prepping is not only satisfying, but also a bit addictive. People may call you a "prepper," but all that truly matters is that you are prepared, come what may.

OUTDOOR LIFE

My Personal First Day of Spring

I stand and look out the back-door window to watch the weather. I see what they call "a mix," raining and snowing at the same time. I have been waiting for spring, waiting for inspiration, yearning for days of warm sunshine. All the seed catalogs have arrived; I haven't looked at them. March Madness, Cabin Fever-- call it what you will-I feel like I have been closed up in this house in the evenings far too long.

I love the return of Daylight-Saving Time, evenings of light that stretch longer each day. But it does not necessarily bring evenings that are warm, or sunny. Winter winds still blow despite the blooming (and now frozen) forsythia, silencing the songs of the spring peepers.

The geese and ducks have returned to the lake out back, but none of them have begun nesting. New songbirds are singing, a vast improvement over Winter's crows, but spring is fickle, and she has not quite yet settled in.

I know, at some point, I'll detect a certain scent in the air and like our beagle, Daisy, I'll turn my face into it and lift my nose to capture it and breathe it in deep. At that moment, I'll feel the warmth of the sun on my face and shoulders and that is the moment that Spring arrives for me. It's the first day of the new season when you cannot, simply cannot stay inside. A day when you can literally hear the activity in the ground around your feet, when you can smell the color green and feel the life within the soil.

Daisy likes to plop herself over and wiggle around on the grass snorting. I always wish I could do that too; she makes it look like it feels so good. And truly, if I'm wearing my work clothes, there's no reason I can't. No reason I can't just toss myself down on the ground and roll around in the grass. It is such a shame I think as a responsible, mature adult, I can't just frolic in the grass. (Perhaps this year I will.)

Though I should do it in the fall, I like to mulch my flower and herb beds in the spring. Not far from one of our beehives, and in the line of traffic from the hive, it is not uncommon for me to rise up from weeding and have a honeybee fly into my face or neck. I make my apologies; I am the one getting in the way. I eventually find myself entranced by the comings and goings of the hive, mesmerized by it as one is by a fish tank, a lava lamp, or a psychedelic screen saver. A few of the bees become interested in the scent of my sweat, and I tell them to go on about their business as I go on about mine.

I've been waiting. Waiting for that day. The day when we gather Winter's debris from the yard and fire up the riding lawnmower to mow down the wild onions that have been sprouting now for weeks. Oh, that fresh and pungent scent.

The next thing you know, I'll buy a sack of peas at the local store and pull out the seeds I saved from last year and drag the seed trays out of the outbuilding. I'll be harvesting chives, shiitake mushrooms, and asparagus, and planting lettuce and more peas (I love fresh peas). I no longer plan a garden--gardens happen here whether you plan them or not. More than once I have sworn I wasn't planting a garden, and we planted the same amount (if not more) as the years we planned it.

Spring instigates it. She whispers, "Just a few seeds here and there."

The first day of spring is not a day on the calendar. It is the day when you throw open all your doors and windows and toss all the floor rugs over the porch handrails. The day you remember, after four months of gray days and red clay mud, why you love these West Virginia hills. A perfect day, when the troubles of the world just evaporate in the sunshine and float away on a soft wind. That is the first day of Spring.

Our Fairweather Friends

During winter months, the big pond behind our house is still and quiet. This winter, it froze over completely, thick enough for Daisy, our beagle, and I to walk across it. For several weeks, the lake existed as a massive hunk of ice - lifeless and cold - much like an empty stage in the theater of our yard. But, with spring's arrival, the cast for this year's wildlife theater are again showing themselves, and the pond is coming back to life again.

The first to make themselves known again were the peeper frogs. I've learned, peepers always freeze their little tushies at least twice. About two weeks ago, I heard a single, solitary peeper, and he didn't have much to say. But this past weekend, we sat on the porch swing and listened to the entire peep-orchestra. I fear this year, they'll get the freeze treatment more than twice.

Second to return are the Canada Geese. I don't think any of these geese we know have ever been to Canada. There's been a pair of geese nesting on the island every year since we moved here in 1999. Since geese live around twenty-four years and mate for life - I assume it's the same pair out there this year.

This year though, is the second year in a row that a second pair of geese want to nest on the island. The territorial disputes are loud and obnoxious and often begin just before dark. They continue off and on all night and keep Frank awake. (I can sleep through almost anything, once I'm asleep.) The original two do well to keep all other geese at bay. Only the second nesting pair seem to have a problem getting the message that they're not wanted.

I'm excited to see the return of ducks. Ducks don't hang out here too often because of the snapping turtles. Last summer, I spent all season watching a quirky little cormorant (looks like a duck, but not a duck), only to witness him disappear below the water one day without so much as a squawk and barely a ripple. I never saw him again and mourned the loss.

The ducks started coming to the water at dusk last fall. I could hear the buzzing of their swift descents above my head when I walked out to close the hen house. Their cooing and light squeals are infinitely more pleasant than the territorial arguments of the geese. All through fall, the ducks came in the evening - but typically in the morning, they were gone. So far this season, we've had six ducks that visit on a regular basis during the day. In the evening, a dozen more or so join them for the night. Only one has decided to stay full-time it seems—a ruddy loner who is more often than not, covered in algae from where he (she?) swims to the bottom for a taste of water greens.

Other birds have returned as well, not just the waterfowl. The bluebirds began building their annual nest in the top of one of our porch posts again—ten feet from the blue birdhouse I bought for them last year. I bought the house in the hope of protecting their young from the sparrows that massacre them annually. For three years, I attempted to return the young to the nest when I found them tossed out onto the porch floor, peeping in the hot sun. But unless I stood watch all day, it was a losing battle, even with my help. The sparrows are relentless.

This year, if the sparrows toss the babies out - they'll have little chance of surviving because a few weeks ago - we got a cat. It's been several years since we've had a cat around here. The loss of Strange Kitty, my feline companion of 20 years, hit me so hard, I hadn't been inclined to replace him. It didn't help that Frank isn't a "cat person." But recently, a local drop-off cat had kittens, and one wandered onto the farm. Once I learned about her, it wasn't long until she living at our house, and named Dandelion. Though she has meals inside, she's mostly an outside cat. Already, I would guess she's cut the local ground mole population in half. At least one sparrow has also fallen prey. When I heard the first killdeer call of the season, I thought, "Oh crap. The cat." Killdeer nest on the ground, and ours have nested smack dab in the center of our vegetable garden several years in a row. I guess that won't be happening this year.

I have a robin I talk with regularly as I sit on the porch swing and he pulls worms from the ground. No, he doesn't talk back, but he does seem to listen. Our pet fowl have gotten livelier as well. The hens follow all groundbreaking tools (shovels, tractor discs, rakes, hoes, tillers) everywhere, sometimes to the threat of their own little lives. Egg production is also up.

It is a pleasure to wake these days to bird song; the winter mornings are so quiet. It's as though friends have risen already and are serenading me awake. Thank goodness, it's finally spring.

The Sounds of Spring

Oh, how I enjoy the sounds of spring. After months of winter silence interrupted only by the rumble of traffic or the caw of crows, the cacophony of spring is truly a celebration of song. First, of course, the spring peepers started. Spring peepers (Pseudacris crucifer) are tan or brown with a dark cross that roughly forms an X on their back (thus the Latin name crucifer, meaning cross-bearer).

I cannot see the frogs, much less their x, without my glasses on, but no one can miss their insistent peeps. Just a few at first, those who awaken too early, the ones who are subdued by the early spring nights that dipped below freezing. Then, as evening temperatures warmed, more and more join the spring call, until their voices are beyond counting, beyond the individual, morphed into an amphibious chorus that lasts all night long. Here, beside the lake, the peepers get so loud they could keep you up at night. For me though, the sound is so soothing, they help me fall right to sleep.

Then, the ducks return. Wood Ducks, Mallards, Bufflehead, Coots, Mergansers. They have little to say during the day, too busy diving and dipping and puttering about. But when they gather on the lake around dusk, zip-lining from the sky to the darkening water's surface, their coos are comforting, yearning, soulful, and serene. Once they return, I begin timing my days so I can wander out onto the back porch at dusk, just to eavesdrop on their conversations and enjoy. Languishing calls in the darkness from one feathered family member to another, coddling calls that seem like sounds of settling, of ruffling off the trials of the day.

German poet Rainer Maria Rilke said, "A birdsong can even, for a moment, make the whole world into a sky within us, because we feel that the bird does not distinguish between its heart and the world's." On the porch glider in the dark, listening to the quibbling ducks, I feel I am a part of their conversation, unable to distinguish between their hearts, the world's, and my own.

The Canada Geese calls are different. Their honks are loud, caustic, annoying. They argue and fight with great frequency, especially when they gather on the water at night. They WILL keep you awake at night, fussing and shouting at each other. Chattering.

By the time the matriarch of the flock sets her nest on the island, the bullfrogs are out of hibernation and add their bass barking to the blend of the spring musical. Their voices push from their throats against the water into the sunlight of the day, into the stillness of the night. Pushing, throbbing, again and again, seeking their mates for the season. Next, the turkeys start mating in the fields, their sporadic gobbles echoing through the valley intermittently throughout the day.

As if these sounds weren't enough, come May, the spring birdsong truly flourishes. We are in a prime location--near water, in the fields, but not far from the edge of the woods. I celebrate the return of each spring bird as thought my friends: the robin, the bluebirds, the red-winged blackbirds. The woodpeckers (red-headed and red-bellied), the American Bittern, the Belted Kingfisher. Shrike, nuthatches, killdeer, titmice.

I sat down one afternoon to simply listen to the song of the catbird and am always listening for the seldom-heard call of the Bob White or the Whippoorwill. Rumi, a Persian poet and Sufi master, once wrote, "Birdsong brings relief to my longing. I am just as ecstatic as they are, but with nothing to say." For me, I feel I have too much to say but cannot find the words. Birds don't need words; they have their songs.

The birdsong at my friend's house in the forest is made up of different songs. The towhee, the vireo, the thrush. She learned the birds and their songs as she grew up here in West Virginia, and she knows them well. I have my grandfather's binoculars, a field guide to birds, the lessons she has taught me, and I try to spy the singers in order to match them in my book. Slowly I learn the birds who tweet, those who warble, those who chit, those who sing.

The last to arrive are the ones who hum, the hummingbirds who come to dive into my iris and spring lilies. They rest briefly in the sassafras tree, shimmering green and aquamarine. As long as I have flowers blooming in my gardens continuously all summer, I have no need to put out a feeder. The hummingbirds visit all season long.

Autumn, I think, is West Virginia's most beautiful time of year visually, but Spring is the loveliest, musically.

Buzzing will come and carry us through summer. The buzzing of wood boring bees determined to hollow out the beams of our back-porch roof. The buzzing of flies, of gnats, of mowers and weed eaters. The buzzing of fans, air conditioners, the rumbling of tractors and tillers, the rip-roaring of ATVs. But, for now, the world is filled with song, glorious music, from brisk mornings into the earthy night. I lie in the lounge chair on the porch in the evenings and just listen, remembering to be still, to be grateful, to breathe.

The Distractions of Nature

I wouldn't call myself a bird watcher. I'm simply a bird witness. It is impossible to live surrounded by trees, grasses, and waters without becoming a bird witness.

Each spring, we begrudgingly and yet anxiously watch to see how many goslings are born and listen for the annoying pierce of the young green herons. In addition, each spring, a bluebird builds her nest at the top of one of the posts that hold up the porch roof.

One morning, while I was folding laundry, I heard a bird ruckus on the porch. Curious, I went to check it out. Of course, all adult birds flew off upon my arrival, but I noticed a newborn baby bluebird on the porch beneath the nest. With gloved hands,

I put it back.

Only moments after I went back inside the house, the ruckus raised again. This time, three of four babies were twitching on the porch--much too young to be attempting their first flights. What was going on here? I put them back, and returned to the house, this time to take watch at the window. Within minutes, three stealthy house sparrows arrived upon the scene. Closer and closer they crept, and together, they attacked. One chased off the bluebird mother, one chased off the bluebird father and the third set upon the nest, pecking the babies' heads and tossing them out on the porch.

I was amazed. Those little sparrows I love to watch hop, hop, hop around my bird feeder in winter had become tiny terrorists in spring. For a while, I stood watch, trying to protect the nest and keep the babies from being tossed out. The laundry could wait a bit. But alas, it was one of the few days the garden was dry enough to work in, and eventually, I had to leave my post.

We needed to plant the melon mounds we had raked up the week before - before we were chased out of the garden by a rainstorm. Arms loaded with a hand shovel and various melon, gourd and cucumber seeds, we headed towards the melon patch where I encountered two Killdeer. The mother had built her nest in one of the unplanted melon mounds. Within the nest lay four eggs. Even so, the other hills needed planting, and this was our chance. Both parents berated us as we worked, feigning injuries to lure us away from the area--a survival tactic that only worked on the dog. Every time we entered the garden, we were subjected to this feathered drama. I began to wonder exactly how long it takes Killdeer eggs to incubate. How long before we could plant our garden in peace?

When I returned from the garden that day, four young bluebirds lie dead on the porch, the parents were gone, and the sparrows were building a nest of their own on the neighboring porch post. I shall never look at sparrows the same way again.

The following day, Frank and I were working in the field, he at one end and me at the other. At one point, from the corner of my eye, I saw him stop working to look up at the sky. I too looked up and saw nothing. From across the field, I heard his voice, "I think those are my bees." Then, I also heard the humming.

A swarm of bees is an amazing thing. Frank dropped his tools and began following the swarm across the field, through and around the hickory tree, into the woods, up the hill--where they settled in a hollow cedar tree. Meanwhile, I headed to the hive, to see if any bees had been inclined to stay.

Our bees had outgrown their hive and divided. We worked that afternoon on methods for gathering the wayward bees and bringing them back to our desired location, our work in the field abandoned.

Then, a Bob White took perch in the tree at the end of the porch. Daisy, our fat, spoiled beagle had settled into her afternoon napping spot when the visitor made its first call. Immediately, Daisy was up, hair raised and growling her way quickly to the porch to see who had invaded her domain. She saw no one. And the visitor called out again. Daisy tipped her head and barked. I let her out and she paced the porch, seeking the stranger in the yard. Again, she saw no one.

Eventually, Daisy laid down across the threshold, protecting the house from the invisible invader. By the time the bird flew off, evening chore time had come, and Daisy had missed her afternoon nap.

On the way out to the chicken house, I passed the pile of unfolded laundry I had abandoned days before to stand guard at the bluebird nest, and I realized, nature is a terrible distraction.

Laundry had been set aside for the battle of the bluebirds. We were short a hill of pumpkins because of the killdeer. The fieldwork remained unfinished because of the bees, and Daisy missed her nap due to the visiting vocal bird.

No wonder it seems like we can't get anything done.

Get Out

A new and growing body of research indicates that direct exposure to nature is essential for healthy childhood development and for the physical and emotional health of children and adults.

In less than one generation's time, millions of Americans have disconnected themselves from nature. The term that describes this disconnect as "nature deficit disorder" was coined by writer Richard Louv in his 2005 book, "Last Child in the Woods."

In his book he notes, "Kids who do play outside are less likely to get sick, to be stressed or become aggressive, and are more adaptable to life's unpredictable turns..." Louv has argued that access to nature is a human right. There was a time when our nation's leaders felt the same way, creating Yellowstone, our first national park, specifically "as a public park or pleasuring-ground for the benefit and enjoyment of the people."

A growing body of research links more time in nature with reduction of stress and depression, faster healing time and less need for pain medication. A few hours in a natural setting increases immunity as well. Other benefits include enhanced use of the senses and higher work productivity.

In 2008, University of Michigan researchers found that an hour interacting with nature improves memory performance and attention spans by 20 percent. In April 2012, researchers at the University of Kansas reported a 50 percent boost in creativity for people who were steeped in nature for a few days.

Several other studies have shown that visiting parks and forests seems to raise levels of white blood cells, including one in 2007 in which men who took two-hour walks in a forest over two days had a 50-percent spike in levels of natural killer cells.

Nature even soothes our brains. Modern multitasking overtaxes brain areas that are involved in suppressing distractions, thinking creatively, and developing a sense of identity. Time outdoors allows those parts of the brain to restore and replenish themselves. In another recent study done in

Scotland, subjects who walked through a rural area viewed their to-do list as more manageable than those who walked on city streets.

Just looking at a natural scene activates parts of the brain associated with balance and happiness. Just looking heightens activity in the anterior cingulate gyrus (which is linked to a positive outlook and emotional stability) and the basal ganglia (an area that's been tied to the recollection of happy memories).

Our inside over-time is making us sick. And as medical folks begin noting that "sitting is the new smoking" in detriment to our nation's overall health, study after study shows that regular time outdoors is good for our bodies, minds, and souls. Our disconnect from nature is detrimental to our bodies and our minds, but it has also separated us from our knowledge and concerns about food, our water, and our air - - all the necessities of life. Millions of Americans have little clue where their food or their water supply comes from. Likewise, we give little thought to what is in the air around and within us.

And while we're sitting in the air conditioning with our digital devices, our rights to nature, clean water, real food, and fresh air - are rights we risk losing. It is high time we start paying attention.

There are real consequences to this growing lack of knowledge about nature and wildlife. We cannot develop a sense of responsibility for nature and wildlife if we know little or nothing about it. We feel little or no responsibility for the source of our own food, air, and water. There are direct corporate efforts to control all three.

Where our recent ancestors had a daily connection to their lands around them, today knowledge of what it takes to manage natural habitats in a world dominated by human influences is seriously undermining conservation efforts. As we disconnect from nature in our daily lives, we care less about it and learn and know less about it. And we're raising generations that know frighteningly little about it - - at a time when our planet needs a world of inhabitants that understand the dynamics of nature and how integral it is to our very existence.

Our disconnect from nature is mutating our bodies, bending our brains and is leading to the destruction of our planet. It is almost unbelievable that so many solutions to so many of our physical, mental, national and world problems are connected to us spending time in our own back yards.

So... Do you want to ease your mind? Lower your blood pressure? Make a connection in your soul? How would you like to help save the planet? You can. Go take a hike.

***

What a pleasure to be able to sit on the porch again! The moment temperatures reached above 50 degrees, I started cleaning off the porch furniture so I could sit and watch the lake, woods, and fields come back to life. I feel as though I can breathe again.

The first day temperatures reached above 60 degrees, Daisy (beagle) and Dandelion (tabby cat) and I walked to the asparagus patch, then to the shiitake mushroom logs, then along our typical strolling path around the lake in our back yard. A goose died in the water over the winter, and we came across the carcass on the bank, picked clean.

In this technological age, our culture has almost forgotten the need for humans to experience the natural environment. We're so busy, so connected, so wound up in our own unnatural worlds that we are losing our own natural ways.

Twenty minutes. Twenty minutes in a natural environment almost instantly improves your body's vitality. The book "Your Brain on Nature" defines vitality as "emotional strength in the face of internal and external oppositions and living life with enthusiasm."

Imagine that. Twenty minutes in nature and you are better able to face challenges and feel perkier about life in general.

Regular exposure to nature affects the body as well. Your immunities are increased, and your body has lower concentrations of cortisol (a stress hormone), lower pulse rate, and lower blood pressure. Studies have shown, just having your desk on the greenery-facing side of an office building and you'll be far less likely to call in sick. Even just looking at landscape posters has been shown to lower stress in people!

And then there's the sunlight. When sunlight hits the skin, it begins a process that leads to the creation and activation of Vitamin D. This vitamin helps prevent osteoporosis and cancer. It also lowers your risk of heart attacks.

So, time outdoors has mental benefits, physical benefits and you know what? Also, spiritual benefits. Being in nature produces brain waves similar to those you experience while meditating or praying.

Wow. I mean WOW. Time in nature is so revitalizing and rejuvenating to our body, mind, and spirit, you would think that we would spend as much time as possible outdoors! But alas, we are instead inside on our couch, at the computer, with our tablets or phones in our hands.

I believe the consequences of our disconnection with nature are beginning to show. We scramble for medications and remediations and anything to make us feel better, and yet we search for fulfillment, comfort, enthusiasm, spiritual relief. We are seeking, seeking - when the solution is all around us.

Here's something to think about: Spending time outside makes you a nicer person. Learning to relate to yourself in the context of the natural world versus "your" world, helps you to empathize with others around you. In this election year, some folks seem they could use a boost of nice. Couldn't we all? Thus, time outdoors also improves the well-being of our relationships, our families and our communities.

Here's another thought: A recent study published in the Journal of Environmental Psychology found that participants who were exposed to nature were more likely to "engage in environmentally sustainable behaviors."

As we spend less time in nature, as children are exposed less and less to nature, we CARE less about the environment. The more time we spend outdoors, the more time children spend outdoors, the more we care about the goose who died, about pollution, about air and water and soil quality. The more time we spend outdoors, the more we will care for our planet.

Make a commitment to get outside, EVERY DAY! Set a goal for 20-30 minutes of simple exposure to nature. You will think, feel and BE better, naturally. It is that easy.

Feathered Friends

The Red-Winged Black Bird and I have become friends this season. He flies down from the pine tree to eat scratch with the hens in the evenings, and his talks to me from the fence posts when I'm in the garden. I call him Red, for short. Each year, he and his family nest in the willows around the edge of the pond out back. This year, the water is higher than usual, and the willows are surrounded by water.

Part of my morning routine includes coffee on the back porch. I watch Read and all the other birds make about their morning business. Swallows skim along the surface of the water, bluebirds swoop back and forth through swarms of gnats and white-winged bugs. The blackbirds and green herons have their typical short flights from the willows to the pines, to the sycamore, and back to the willows.

One morning, Red and his family were darting down at the water's surface, scolding and squawking and making one heck of a fuss. From my perch on the porch, I couldn't quite see what upset them so on the water's surface. I reached for the binoculars.

To my dismay, I realized what was happening. Two of their young had apparently attempted their first flight from the nest - - and had ended up in the water. They were attempting to fly, wings out and flapping, but weighed down by the dropping liquid weight. One had made it halfway across the water to the island, and one had paddles three-quarters across.

In an instant, I was up and across the yard in my bare feet, shoving the canoe into the water. In less than a minute, I reached the nearest victim. It quit struggling when the canoe came near it, and I scooped it effortlessly out of the water as we glided by. It clung to my fingers tightly, and the time it took to get it to let go and land on the floor of the canoe got me out of alignment to reach the other struggling bird easily. I had to make a hard turn back left, and would either run over it or be too far to reach it by hand. I chose the latter and tried to scoop it up with my paddle. It had apparently been in the water longer than the other and was too exhausted to help itself balance on the paddle's plastic. I had to back paddle and twist a little far, but I finally managed to grab it up from the water.

The fledgling had no strength to even cling to me, and I just held it close, canoe floating on the water. For the moment, the emergency had passed. Red and his wife were scolding me, still darting back and forth above my head. I set the little one down next to its sibling and paddled back to the yard.

I kept the rescues both in my lap in the back-porch glider at first, both still soaking wet, and the cat too close for comfort. Eventually, the cat wandered off as cats do, unaware of what I held protectively in my lap, and I placed both little birds on an eye-level branch of the Sycamore tree near the back porch where I could keep watch on them. Not long after, one of them began to peep, peep, peep - - and Red and his mate came to comfort and encourage their young.

At that point, I would already be late for work, so I left them in their parents' care. Before I left, I looked out at the Sycamore again, and the two had both hopped their way to higher branches. When I came home from work, there were chores to do, and then a typical evening walk with a friend. We were sitting in the back porch swing afterward, and I heard Red and his wife in the Sycamore, still chirping out encouraging commands. I grabbed the binoculars and spied one of the young survivors on a thin branch, high in the top of the tree. The momma kept chirping and chirping and soon enough -- the young one took flight across the yard and around the corner into the side yard pine.

Since I am overly aware of the wildlife around us, I'm amazed when human visitors come to our porch swing and spend time - oblivious to all the happenings right before them. It is important for us to stay aware of our environment, to keep that connection with the land that we <should be> bound to care for and respect. If you stay aware of the wildlife around you, you are bound to come across an opportunity to help.

We Are Nature

I love the way thunder rolls across the sky, how it rumbles in your bones at the first boom, then ripples, grumbling past the eastern hillside and on across the horizon. As children, we would watch for the flashes of lightning, like watching for fireworks, and count as we were taught to determine the distance to the strike. One, one thousand. Two, one thousand. But now, I am happy to listen to the rain and the thunder as the sky chastises the earth.

Today, a storm crossed overhead, with consistent rumbling for nearly half an hour. Instantly, the heat of the afternoon lifted. Rain fell steady, but not pounding, and ground drank it in. I spent as much time as I could on the back porch in the glider, as porches are made for storm watching. You can experience the storm and be exposed to it but remain dry and relatively safe.

After the storm passed, wisps of fog swirled up from the valley, moisture drawn up into the system, just to be dropped back down somewhere else. From the valley to the hilltop perhaps, to keep the cycle turning. Once the storm moved on, its grumble fading as it wandered across the atmosphere, the setting sun raised temperatures again, and new wisps rose and swirled. The orange light shone more than usual, heightened by the moist reflections of everything just washed clean.

Nothing matches a summer evening after an afternoon thunderstorm in the hills of Appalachia. I feel as though I am inside a terrarium, the moisture dripping down from a giant glass dome above. Sometimes, life here feels sealed inside a bubble, secluded from the rest of the world. Sometimes stifling hot and sweaty, sometimes baking, parched and dry, sometimes fresh and clean and sparkling.

As the skies cleared, and the water temperatures on the lake out back balanced, I watched the green duckweed expand again across the face of the water, no longer compressed by rippling waves, and a mother deer appeared on the bank of the island, and a fawn so wobbly that had to be out for its very first walk. With the rumbling over, bird song started again, and the chickens and the robins pecked in the saturated yard for earthworms and bugs. And in that moment, the fields around me and time itself seemed to expand, and the concerns of the world shrank to a pittance.

I felt relief. Relief from the heat of the day, relief from the stress of the week, relief in knowing there are still magical moments in this world- the way nature can make us feel small and immense at the same time, connected when we are or feel alone. Humans have forgotten that we ARE nature. We are hard-wired to benefit from exposure to it. We get Vitamin D from the sun (statistically, the average American is Vitamin D deficient), and multiple studies show that 20 minutes in nature can lower blood pressure, relieve stress, depression, and anxiety. We are not technical, mechanical creatures. We are (or were?) natural creatures. Writer Laurence G. Boldt says, "a society at odds with nature is a society at odds with itself."

After the recent summer storm passed, I contemplated why that moment was reassuring, comforting. How that moment "outside" of society, disconnected from man but connected to nature, could soothe my spirit so. And again, I remembered something Boldt says in his book, *Zen and the Art of Making a Living*. He said, "Society can be interested in a man or woman only as a political or economic entity; a culture is interested in more... Cultures care for their peoples as natural, spiritual beings and not simply as workers or consumers." In other words, humans are not just political, economic beings. We were meant for more than work and consumption. We are nature, spiritual, but we live in a society that neither acknowledges, values, nor endorses us as such.

Boldt says, "Our whole effort is to gain and hold, acquire and defend." The American approach to life and living is a mindset typically used for warfare. We are focused on getting-striving, consuming, keeping, maintaining--status, power, reputation, cars, houses, etc.--no matter the cost to our own well-being or the natural world around us. Americans live with a mentality to conquer and defend. No wonder we're so stressed.

I believe this is why time in nature is so soothing to the soul. Nature is the ultimate level playing field. Nature doesn't care about status, reputation, shoes, or the latest cell phone app. Social media, television series, all our little rat race games and power struggles are irrelevant. Our narcissism, prejudices, irrational judgments, daytime dramas, are insignificant. And if anything, that's a relief.

Boldt says, "We cannot be fully awake, fully alive, fully human--and remain indifferent to the world in which we live." The costs of denial and suppression are devastating to human happiness and creativity. Boldt notes, until our society changes its consideration humans as nothing more than workers and consumers, "it will continue to take uncommon courage, strength, and perseverance for individuals to realize meaning in their everyday experiences."

When we stop and take a time out with nature around us, Boldt says, "the mind is arrested and raised above desire and loathing... the contemplation of beauty eliminates selfish desire." In turn, "Ugliness depresses and diminishes life--sapping the creative spirit of the individual and weakening the character of society." Did you get that? Ugliness saps creativity and weakens our character. No wonder the beauty of the hills after a storm provided me with such relief. How lucky we are to live where the natural beauty around us can soothe our souls.

Wild Neighbors

I've come to feel as though I know every bird, frog, deer, duck around us. Many are like summer tourists, returning each year -and we've come to know and notice when they come and go. For example, I know that our local peeper frogs always freeze twice once they start singing in early spring.

The killdeer have laid their ground nest in our garden the last three years in a row. (Their show entertained us the first year, but the dramatics grew annoying the years after that.)

We watch the geese who nest on the island defend the water around it each year and have observed some extremely violent altercations between the male goose and any other goose that attempts to visit the water once the eggs have been laid. And we watch, once the eggs hatch, different goose couples rally back around each other so they can teach and protect the goslings as a group - all previous in-fighting all but forgotten.

This year, we have baby ducks too. They're so much more entertaining than the geese (and don't make such a nasty mess.) Ducks don't nest around here often. The goslings may be too big for a snapper to take under easily - but a baby duck can disappear in an instant without so much as a ripple on the water. The snapper got my friend the cormorant this year (looks kinda like a duck but isn't a duck). I've been watching him paddle, bob, and swim around for two years, and I miss him nearly every day.

I know of at least one BIG snapping turtle and one big soft-shell turtle in the pond - I watch them return in the spring too. They come up through the drainage ditches through the hay fields from the creek in the spring and cross the yard to the lake along the exact same path every year. This year though, the soft shell was off about 10 yards and it got blocked in under the back porch. Had I not heard it scratching and carried it out to the water myself, it's hard to tell how long the turtle's instincts would have kept it attempting to climb that wall.

We also have an unsolved turtle mystery. When we first started gardening, we put some horse manure in a 50-gallon tub and filled it with water. We then used this "manure tea" to fertilize gardens and plants.

Following the first year though, it weakened with the rain waters, and so it was left, mostly forgotten, under a shade tree outside the garden fence. A few years later, we had a get together in the side yard, and sitting around, I kept hearing a scratching sound behind me under the shade tree. When I went to investigate, found a snapping turtle, about eight inches across - - swimming around in that drum of water! Its back was black with algae, so it had to have been in there for a good while. I can't imagine how that turtle got in there! Can you?

Feeling sorry for it, I scooped it out of that barrel and carried it to the lakeside. I didn't want it in there, but I also felt compelled to at least let it experience a bigger world than it had ever known.

When we were quietly floating around the pond on our rafts a few weeks ago, that turtle surfaced about twenty feet away from me and stayed there, looking my direction, for about five minutes. I think that was my thank-you.

This year, I decided to buy a blue birdhouse. For three years in a row, I have watched the bluebirds build their nest at the top of one of the porch posts - and three years in a row, I have seen the sparrows come and attack the parents then throw the young ones out of the nest onto the porch floor in the blazing sun. So, I bought a sparrow-proof blue birdhouse and mounted it next to their favorite porch post. They built on the porch post anyway, and the sparrows came and tore apart the nest. I stuffed paper into the space where the nest had been, so they couldn't build there again. They rebuilt on a different post. So, then I stuffed paper into the space above EVERY porch post. I did not see them at all for weeks. Then a storm came and blew down the paper above one post - and two days later the bluebirds were building there again. I think it's a little late now in the season for them to lay eggs, so I hope the nest is safe.

I've been told it may take them several years before they adopt the house I bought for them. It frustrates me because the sparrow raid is violent and upsetting for all of us. But I can't force them to move into the condo I bought for them. I'll just have to wait to see if they ever decide to on their own.

The most exciting episode by far this year happened earlier this week. I was moving towards the far end of our upper garden when I spooked a deer hiding in the nearby brush. She bolted, down along the back side of the pond where she had to leap over a coyote who had come out of the woods to get a drink. The coyote wasn't fazed a bit by the near-miss and headed on back to the woods. The deer, however, did not continue on, sensing a threat. She got about 35 yards past the coyote and stopped, stepping cautiously and keeping her tail in the air.

I thought it odd she did not keep running, but then remembered – she had tucked her little one away on the island. Every morning they wade across the shallow side to the island and the mother leaves the little one there. That's why she did not continue running. She was checking the threat to her young, not herself.

It is amazing how much local wildlife can become a part of our lives. When winter comes, I hate to see many of our friends leave. In spring, I celebrate their return. During the summer we truly enjoy them - these wild neighbors of ours.

Peaceful, But Not Quiet

Frank and I have a big mattress size inflatable raft we use to float around on the pond in our back yard. We used to drive to Bee Run at Sutton Lake on a regular basis, but then we started a garden, and then we started this magazine and - well, we just don't have the time as we used to for those all-day runaways. With our raft and the pond though, we can shove off the bank and float in the sun for a lazy hour or two, with zero travel time, and be far enough away to not hear the phone ring.

When you are floating on the water like that, between a wooded hillside and a field of hay, half asleep in the sunshine, you listen. You listen to the constant crescendo of the katydid's leg scratchings, the buzz of passing horseflies, the far-off roar of a passing plane. The insect song begins with those at ground level, but comes from clear up the hillside, far above our head, from tucked under rocks and perches on tree bark. People who visit our back porch say, "It's so quiet here," and I think, "this isn't quiet, it's a chorus."

Quiet comes in January when the only sound you hear is your own breath and heartbeat.

Lazy August afternoons in the country are louder than you think, if you listen. Hundreds of insects grate their legs together, flap their wings to express their lives, their existence. But it is peaceful, the insect song, the music that runs through the day between morning and evening birdsong. Funny how easily our minds dismiss this massive orchestra as background noise. But, if you focus on the layers of their songs, tune in to as you float suspended on still water, the clutter in your mind just fades away.

Hear the locust in the nearby willow tree, the cricket in the tall grasses at the water's edge. Hear others calling back to them from the maple in the yard, the rock face on the hillside, from blades of grass across the hay fields. Hear the clicking of dragonfly wing as a pair flying past try to join each other.

Often, I read on the back porch in my favorite fold-out lounge chair. Without looking up, I know the hum of the hummingbird, the buzz of a bumblebee from that of a wood-boring bee from that of a honeybee or wasp or yellowjacket. I know the sound of a horsefly caught in a spider's web. I think all outdoor inclined folks know the buzz of the dreaded horsefly, who is fortunately fat and slow enough to be swatted. I believe most country folks know the sound of the mosquito, buzzing at your ear.

Every summer, a black cricket moves into our basement kitchen and sings from underneath our refrigerator. This is supposed to be good luck, but he chirps at night -which gives a true perspective to the volume of his voice. I can't crunch bugs - but I have attempted to catch him by covering him with a mason jar to transport him back to his natural surroundings. But he's too quick for the jar, and thus still serenades the kitchen appliances all night long.

While mowing last week, I brushed under a low-hanging pine branch and covered my arms and legs with debris. I looked down at my hands on the mower's steering wheel and I almost missed it, a tiny walking stick (that's an insect) gangly and fragile, moving slowly across my hand. It is the first I've seen of one since the late 1990s. I wondered how many of these silent creatures hatched this year, how many were alight in that pine tree? How much life is out there, life we don't even consider or worse yet, dismiss?

I will miss this "noise" come winter. I will miss the constant insect song and even the nightly cricket serenade. I dread that sterile silence of cold days when the insects are all buried or frozen and gone. But this afternoon, we'll float in it. We'll paddle ourselves out onto the water and soak ourselves in the insect sounds of life around us. We'll bask in their song and the sun and enjoy our lazy summer hour or so before the summer is gone.

Savoring the Season

I walk through the yard in my bare feet (something I rarely do) to stand and stare at a patch of goldenrod that took over one corner of my herb garden. Yes, I am allergic to goldenrod, and fall allergies this year have just been miserable. But I can't help it. The goldenrod is bustling with activity, literally covered with hundreds of insects relishing in its golden glory. Honeybees, bumblebees, wasps, hornets, beetles, sweat bees, butterflies. All the pollinators in one place. I stand and watch, not just for the awareness of an entire insect world in a concentrated space, but also just to feel the warmth of the sun on my arms and my face, to feel the damp itchy grass under my feet and between my toes.

After hanging silent most of August, my windchime is pleasantly active again, ringing the tones of Big Ben throughout the day in the autumn breezes. Katydids and coyote are the prominent calls of the night, but the owls have been more outspoken as of late, and the ducks call more soulfully in the darkness it seems.

Autumn. Spring stirs my heart, but not as deeply as autumn. Spring is a time of beginnings; autumn is a time of endings. The days already are growing shorter, and I need a blanket or a jacket to sit on the porch now most nights. The woods smell musky and rich, a scent that will enhance before the falling leaves dry to a crunch.

The insects on the goldenrod collect the pollen in a frenzy, instinctually driven by the same calling that drew me outside to begin with. The knowledge that winter is coming and time for absorbing and gathering in the warm sun is limited. Milkweed has almost gone to seed, and garden harvests are mostly managed by now except for the late-season pumpkins, peppers, and squash. Hay is cut and baled, and the hills are sporting colors besides their verdant summer green.

Daisy, our fat beagle who spends the heat of summer napping on the cool concrete floor in the basement, is excited to take walks again now that the temperatures are more tolerable. She likes to roll in the leaves and the grasses and grunt with pleasure in such a way that I am tempted to drop down on the ground and roll around some myself. Dandelion, our cat, wanders from the path when she gets curious, then races to catch up with us when we've gotten too far ahead.

I sliced the last garden-fresh tomato remaining on my counter with a certain sadness. Although their goodness has been collected in jars, it simply is not the same as fresh-sliced from local soil. Back to store-bought tomatoes that refuse to ripen. I will miss fresh tomatoes and the grass between my toes.

Autumn is the most beautiful time of year, and no one in West Virginia can deny the magic of the mountains and hills once the leaves start to turn. I cannot help but take every opportunity to examine each phase of the kaleidoscopic color changes while walking barefoot through the yard, commuting to work, or sitting in the glider on the back porch. I love West Virginia this time of year.

This is a time of honey and molasses, of stuffed squashes, pumpkin pies, and apple cider. Jacket season, when the socks come out again. When you need a blanket when hanging out on the couch, but don't yet want to turn any heat on in the house.

I always feel these days are rich with satisfaction, with the knowledge that summer, the season of production and activity, was well spent. Flowers and vegetables produced, new generations born, cycles successfully continued.

I see some gardens are already cleared, emptied and fallow and waiting for winter in preparation for the cultivation of new seeds and plants come spring. I find myself reflecting and ruminating on the season passing, but also planning for those yet to come.

Rubber Boots & Muddy Tulips

As I sit to write this, fewer than 60 days remain until spring. Of course, with these mild winter temperatures, my tulips and lilies began sprouting a week ago, in January.

I dislike West Virginia winters that don't include a good amount of snow. As every country dweller knows, without cold temperatures and snow--the whole world grows soft with mud.

I refer to the time from February to April as "Mud Season." It's that time a year when everything around you goes soggy, when that dry, hard driveway of summer becomes a boggy, sloppy path. The time of year when a walk to the chicken coop is accentuated with "squish, squish, squish" the entire way. With snow, I might tiptoe across the yard in my green garden clogs, but with all the mud, rubber boots are a must. Santa brought me a new pair of blue rubber boots this Christmas after my rainbow-daisy-covered pair sprung a leak at the ankle. I stepped into the lake's edge to grab hold of the canoe, and my right boot filled with water. I might be able to patch them, but I'll never fully depend on them again.

I bought my first pair of "adult" rubber boots after I experienced the first floodwaters here on the farm, when I waded waist-deep up our driveway, watched as a round hay bale floated by me. That pair of boots had pull-on loops at the top of the boot, and more than once I hooked bungee cords from the outside loop on the boot to the belt loops on my pants to keep them from being sucked off my feet by the mud.

A country girl must have rubber boots--and I wear mine most often in February and March. I have a goal to walk every day-a goal I don't meet often enough. But when I do, I slip on my blue rubber boots and Daisy Dewdrop, our beagle, and I squish our way around the lake, across the fields, meandering at Daisy's pace, stopping to sniff at interesting things all along the way. When she was younger, she would run ahead of me and I would struggle to keep up in my rubber boots, but we are older now, and the lazy stroll is good enough.

In the words of Wendell Berry, "When despair for the world grows in me... I come into the peace of wild things who do not tax their lives with forethought of grief. I come into the presence of still water..."

Daisy and I are not walking for the exercise, we are walking for the peace of wild things. We're walking to shake off too much sitting, to unplug and disconnect. She's walking to sniff out her world and see what's been intruding, I'm walking to let go of the intrusive concerns of mankind, to balance myself by returning to a more natural perspective of life.

Our lazy strolls are relaxing (and certainly needed), but I prefer to walk through snow than mud. The world is more hushed, pristine and peaceful. Snow is so beautiful and relaxing. Mud--is mud. It is slippery, it stains, it seeps and sloshes.

Daisy too prefers snow over mud. In the snow, she is friskier, livelier, and the white of her face seems less obvious on the white background. But in the mud, she steps gingerly, dainty and delicate, knowing she'll wear any major splashes on her belly and backside. When we return home, she spends extra time cleaning her legs and feet after I've toweled them off.

On today's walk, I found an abandoned turtle shell, and Daisy waded into the lake's edge to slurp big gulps of fresh water. I noticed my tulips sprouting already, and some of the lilies. A few of our honeybees were buzzing around the outside trash cans. Sights of spring in late January, fresh life that will likely be frozen when the weekend temperatures drop again.

Those with cold frame gardens are surely being blessed currently with kale, carrots, even perhaps hardy lettuces, or even broccoli. Each year I hope to start a winter garden, and each fall I'm so worn out by the summer garden, the winter garden has yet to happen. But, the sight of the tulips and some lily sprouts makes me wonder about the asparagus--if it will also be popping up early. Makes me think about planting peas.

I do hope for more cold and snow before spring arrives. I hope for a winter that feels like winter. A serious dose of pristine white that solidifies mud, turns the squishing to crunching, one that frosts the tips of the tulips. One more fat, fluffy snowfall that continues for a full day and night. One that lingers for days before melting away.

I hope for a cold snap that kills bugs, a snowfall that forces me to wear my snow boots, soft-lined and snuggly, especially compared to my blue rubber boots. I hope I can go from snow boots to garden clogs and skip over all this mud.

Surely winter can't be over yet.

Not All the World is Mud

When most people think of February, they typically think of valentines and love. My view of February follows along the same line as the historical Anglo-Saxons, who referred to this month as "Solmoneth" which means, "mud month."

Mud. I hate mud. I'd rather have below-freezing temperatures, ten inches of snow and no electric for five days than an entire month of mud. Mud is like the flu--if you are anywhere around it, it gets on you, on all your stuff, and goes with you wherever you go. And much like the flu, it seems you can't go anywhere without running into it.

Especially in February, those little matters in life that get you down also act like mud. Mean people, struggles, disappointments-- these incidents splash "mud" on your mind, and if you let them, they alter your mood. In that mood, that mud floats around in your brain, coming in contact with your outlook on other situations, spreading the mud on them and getting them dirty as well. Pretty soon, you don't have a single pair of shoes or a thought in your head that isn't tainted by mud month.

Around here, it is quite a challenge to keep from getting muddy. Feed the chickens... Mud. Take out the trash... Mud. Walk the dog... Mud. Get in and out of the car... Mud.

Likewise, it is sometimes difficult to avoid that mental mud, negativity. Gossip, judgment, prejudice, jealousy, complaining, insecurity--all of these are mental mud. As it is with red clay mud, so it is with mental mud. We must work at keeping that negativity creeping into our heads and contaminating everything.

One of my favorite sayings is, "you can wallow around in the mud, or you can stand up and walk out of it." As much as it may seem that mud is everywhere, there are places that are mud free. For mental mud, these mud-free places are found among positive friends and loved ones, discovered in the search for community solutions.

As much as it may seem that mud is never-ending, there is more time in our lives without mud than with it. The mud does not exist when our world is white and frozen, and the mud will not last past the spring rains into the heat of summer. Red clay may thrive around us forever, but its soggy state is only temporary.

It's when we stand around in the mud, stomping our feet and keeping it wet with our tears that we become stuck. When we wallow in self-pity, blame our problems on others and respond in anger and fear, we make more mud.

An integral part of rural life is maintaining the fight against red clay mud. An integral part of a happy life is keeping up the fight against mental mud. This we can do by not wallowing in it with others, by leaving the problems of the world at the door, taking responsibility for solving problems ourselves, and endlessly working to focus on the good, and not the bad in life.

Sure, right now it is muddy. It's February, and it is the season of mud. Be kind. No matter what the groundhog says, spring is just around the corner, holding the promise of new color, new color, new life, and not-so-soggy ground.

The Comfort of Nature

I have been grateful for the unseasonably sunshiny days, though they worry me some as well. Our active honeybees have nothing to eat, and the tulips grew six inches tall and survived an overnight freezing snow--only to be eaten by a deer because I haven't replaced the garden fences I took down last fall to more easily clean the beds.

I am a worrier. The current conditions in our nation and in our planet are enough to drive a worrier completely insane. I hide from national and world news and my nine-year Facebook addiction has finally been cured. I can go more than 24 hours now and log on for less than five minutes (if I'm on a high-speed connection).

I also still have those prepper tendencies and beliefs: the importance of self-reliance, of local sources and networks, of community, neighbors, holistic health and simple living. I spent nearly eight years getting ready to just hunker down.

Some days, I just have to put on my mud boots, call to our beagle Daisy, and walk around the lake and fields to remind myself that the sky isn't actually falling. It may be filling with carbon, but the sky this week has been blue and beautiful, the sun bright and warm on my face. It may be far too early, but some of the trees are beginning to bud, and the peepers have started to sing. The ground is extremely wet and mushy, but I can smell the soil, that earthy scent that seeps up from every squishy step.

Nothing relaxes me like outside time in the sunshine. I realize, technically, my body is soaking up Vitamin D in an attempt to correct the current season's deficit, but I cannot help but simply raise my face up to the sun's glorious warmth and brightness and let out a massive, purging sigh.

I spent an hour clearing and prepping the asparagus and herb beds, sloughing off my jacket, and then simply sat in a chair in the yard for twenty minutes, soaking up the sun and watching our honeybees fly to and fro in search of food. We'll have to supplement their diet, and I'll have to get those fences back up around the remaining tulips and the lilies that have started to show, and the world does certainly seem to have gone insane sometimes. And with a twenty-minute dose of bright, warm, sunshine, I feel as though I can manage it.

I cannot tell if my current frumpiness is tied to the current political conditions on our state/ nation/world, or is related to the natural condition many people suffer this time of year, Seasonal Affective Disorder (SAD). SAD comes from that lack of sunlight, that drop in Vitamin D, a contributor to serotonin, the body's natural mood stabilizer. Perhaps my tension and lack of energy are due to my current work schedule, adapting to the current transitions in my life.

In the end, I find myself discussing stress, depression, fatigue, frustration, aches, and pains with many of my friends. I am not the only one feeling the effects of our nation's upheaval. For that's the point of it. No matter what your political, environmental, social or religious sentiments, as a nation, we have been upheaved. The only place I find I can truly feel settled and grounded again is outside, in the sunshine.

While I do hope winter has not yet finished with us (I'd like to see more bugs frozen), I am grateful for these shining not-quite-spring days. And for a few minutes, I can let myself not worry about the apple and pear blossoms being frozen, the state of our state, or the state of the nation. For a brief moment in the sunshine, with birdsong and bees buzzing, I can feel peace and comfort that at that moment, life is beautiful and good.

PURPOSEFUL LIFE

Bemoan, or Be Blessed

Frosty nights have come, fallen leaves and browning grass crispy white in the mornings. I need a blanket now to have my morning tea on the porch. The summer songbirds have migrated away, and the milkweed has gone to seed. I've tucked away my flip flops and open-toe shoes. My sock drawer is active again. So long skin-baring tank tops, comfy cut-offs. Days start now with sleeves and jackets, but soon these layers are shed once the work starts; clearing the garden, prepping the chicken pen for winter, weed eating one last time.

This time of year makes me anxious and melancholy. I'm anxious over the summer chores yet left undone, melancholy because I know, all too soon, I will be spending weeks indoors separated from the porch, the pond, the grass, the woods, and fields.

Already the winds have kicked up, in chill and emphasis. The new wind chime I bought in lazy summer rings out now more than ever. The forsythia branches grew so much this summer the winds now have them scratching and beating on the outside of the bedroom wall. They too seem anxious and melancholy.

I make a point in November, like many others around the world, to think about all the things I am grateful for. I try to spend extra time in the porch swing, extra time outdoors in the sun and fresh air. I try to focus on the insect song, the sound of breezes through crisping leaves.

Already I feel the urge to hibernate, to go to sleep and not wake up until spring. Of course, there's far too much to do. I remind myself how fortunate I am, to work on projects I enjoy, to be earning my MFA, to be warm and fed and loved. I am grateful for every drama-free day, pain-free day, stress-free day. I have a friend who reminds me, "If nothing truly terrible happened today, then it's been a pretty good day."

Seems as though we live in a culture of complaint. We moan about anything that isn't picture perfect. And yet when I think of those who have lost loved ones, who have been hungry, or have lost their health, their source of income, I realize how blessed I am.

On social media, November is often a time when people celebrate "Thirty Days of Thanksgiving" in which every day we acknowledge something or someone we are grateful for. I participated in this two or three years ago and awakened to all the many blessings in my life. In fact, by the end of the month, I felt nearly embarrassed, almost boastful, once I realized how truly blessed I am.

If we are warm, safe, healthy and not hungry or thirsty, we are blessed. Too many people in this state, nation, the world do not have these necessities. Life is a blessing, one that many are denied every day.

Though November may have already started by the time you read this, start your list of blessings today, adding to your list each day. By the time we reach Thanksgiving at the end of the month, you should be fully aware of your blessings and all those things you should be grateful for.

There's a reason we're told to count our blessings. The practice provides us with a perspective of gratitude and joy. Start counting.

Learning to be Still... And Ordinary

I fear the season for porch sittin' has nearly reached its end. The cattails are puffed and shaggy, the garden has passed its prime and the fields are cleared for winter. Autumn has always been my favorite time of year, but I rarely welcome it with the excitement I do spring. There is a period in fall, a brief pause between summer chores and the holiday bustle when the hills about us seem to say, "just rest for a minute." New colors appear on the leaves each day, new scents arrive on the now-daily breezes. What a shame not to stop our hustle and bustle to appreciate the beauty that abounds.

I believe there is therapy in time spent with nature. However, I have never learned to 'be still.' I always feel I should be doing something. Lord knows, there's plenty that needs done. Being still though, is an important skill to develop. It is when we are still that we can appreciate the world around us. It is when we are still we take account of our blessings, large and small. When we are still, our mind can catch up with all the small joys our schedule rushed us through.

When we are still, we are at rest. Body, mind, and spirit at rest. Some people call it meditation, but I think a moment of stillness in nature is more than that. It is a well-spring, a rejuvenating moment if you can be still long enough to let it flow through you. The smell of the leaves fills your body with richness, the breeze comes by to raise your chin and lift your face to the sun. And for that moment, you suddenly feel fortunate. You feel blessed, and you feel that all is well.

I find it is easier to be still somewhere away from home, where the phone, chores, everyday worries aren't so obvious. But it is amid all our worries that we need to learn to relax and count our blessings. It is when we are busy that we are disconnected from that feeling of comfort and sense of place.

* * *

I recently attended a memorial service for my aunt and uncle who, married 63 years, died one week apart. During their service, they were celebrated as ordinary people--what used to be ordinary. It used to be ordinary to be married for life. It used to be ordinary to live to serve your spouse, your family, your community, church, country, with quiet honor and joy. It used to be ordinary to love and trust freely with all your heart and soul. Ordinary used to be defined as "usual or normal."

My aunt and uncle, in many ways, represented a generation of ordinary that will soon be lost.

These days, everyone wants to be special. Everyone wants to be recognized as something more than ordinary. But through their simple ordinary lives based on honor, love, faith, and family, Aunt Betty and Uncle Bob became extra-ordinary in the eyes of all who knew and loved them.

Bob and Betty were truly, "the salt of the earth." But these days, who celebrates salt? It is so ordinary; such a small thing.

There were days, in Biblical times, when salt was considered quite a valuable mineral, a commodity for trading in the marketplace. But these days, simple folks and simple pleasures are often over-shadowed by star-studded "real life" celebrities and the newest upgrade. No longer do we aspire to be salt. These days, the world wants "hot and spicy" or "sweet and sour" or, at the very least, "new and improved."

We've lost our appreciation for the once steadfast ordinary. Instead, we try to measure value and worth by counting only the extra perks of our lives.

Being still is learning to reconnect with the ordinary—to see it, appreciate it, and be thankful for it. Being still is a special skill that allows us to appreciate the blessings of ordinary lives. While my aunt and uncle knew how to keep busy, they also both knew how to be still.

The world tends to make us feel small. But when we are still in some of the world's most beautiful natural settings, we can easily appreciate the ordinary. The sounds of the birds singing; the bright colors of the leaves in fall, the babbling brook.

When we are still, we can likewise reflect on the ordinary accomplishments of simple living: a garden harvested, a field cut, a stack of firewood in its ordinary place along the cabin wall. None of these in passing seem special. But in the autumn, if you are still, and simply absorb the abundance of the ordinary that surrounds you, you may discover an extra-ordinary feeling of joy and peace.

Aunt Betty and Uncle Bob knew how to appreciate the small blessings. They knew the joy of giving and the pleasure of serving others. They experienced a lifetime of love.

May we all be so ordinary.

* * *

We rush through our lives trying to prove we have worth, that we are special. The truth is, if we are still, we can appreciate the ordinary, and come to realize that we already are special to those we love and who love us.

Every day, we make a difference, be it large or small. Most of the time, it is the consistent, small fascinations. Those everyday ordinary incidents over time make the biggest difference of all. The color of the leaves on the trees in the autumn may be an ordinary part of life, but this display only comes once a year. If you are still, you will even notice that the colors vary from year to year due to changes in the weather and water levels in the ground.

If you bustle through life and don't take the time to appreciate the beauty, the next time you look, the leaves will have fallen, and the colors of the mountains will all be gone. What you dismissed as ordinary will, in its absence, leave the winter world brown and grey.

Do not dismiss the ordinary. Be still and appreciate the small details we overlook each day. You may discover, in the end, you are extraordinarily blessed.

Clearing the Path for Laughter

I like people who laugh easily. I love big, belly-laughers. I like people who make me laugh because I am not a person naturally prone to laughter. I wish I was. I can sit in a pub, restaurant or room of people, and smile with their laughter, and think one of two things:

1. What lightness of being do they have that allows them to laugh so freely?

2. I don't get it. Was that funny?

It's not that I don't have a sense of humor. I do. (I'm pretty sure I do.) It's just that my sense of humor is dry, sarcastic, and often--only funny to me. I think it is because my personality--in its natural state--is dry and sarcastic.

I can remember laughing easily--because around certain people, I still do. But somewhere between being a child and a "mature, responsible adult," my natural state of mind is more humor-challenged. High school, college, four years of waitressing, bad relationships, three years as a reporter dealing with small-town politics--you can imagine how anyone of these experiences can sap the humor out of life. However, I found it troubling to discover that the culmination of these experiences had permanently shifted my "natural" state of mind.

And it was nowhere near funny—unless you take a sarcastic look at it all.

Our decision to simplify our lives, raise our own foods, give up network television, create a sustainable lifestyle--was to find our way back being who we wanted to be. We didn't want to be frantic and cluttered. We didn't want to eat "pseudo" foods, we didn't want to be pelted every day with propaganda, negativity.

We wanted work that immersed us in learning, better living, a slower pace. Tasks that allowed for creativity, personal development, expression, practicality. We wanted to create a life that made us people who laugh easily. All of this is a long term, slow-going process and we may, or may not, succeed.

We recently remodeled our kitchen. I think it is actually called "upcycling" because we didn't use anything purchased new, but it certainly is more organized and user-friendly. Because everything (and I mean

EVERYTHING) had been moved, it took some time for me to adjust to the new places and locations of kitchen tools and ingredients. Within a few days, I had mostly adapted.

However, weeks later, I still found myself standing where the trash can used to be. Again and again, I found myself in that spot, hands full of dripping meat wrappers or crumb-filled paper towels or something of the like - and no container was there.

Eliminating sarcasm and negativity from your life is a lot like moving the kitchen trash can. Out of habit, you go to the former location, even though you don't want to go there anymore. Only after you find yourself standing with your hands full of garbage, do you realize (again) that you are in the wrong place (again).

We formerly kept the trash can in the front room. Everyone who came to the house had to pass it, and you had to leave the kitchen to get to it. In other words, everyone could see where we kept our garbage, and to get it there, we had to go out of the way of the cooking processes.

Sarcasm and negativity are the same. Everyone can see them, and they take you away from the process of living a happy life.

Now the trash can has its own covered cubby, next to the kitchen sink. It's hidden, convenient, and near the water to wash your hands clean when you've emptied them. No mess, no open drama, no residual issues or distractions from the real task at hand.

That's practical living. The garbage of our life is collected properly, round-filed, and disposed of quickly and cleanly. It may not be funny, but it is certainly an improvement.

The frustration, distraction, that once came with the garbage no longer detracts from a natural state of being. No longer shifts the mindset towards the sarcastic and away from joy.

If you've ever seen a baby's natural tendency to laugh and play, you cannot deny that joy and happiness, in the beginning, is a natural state of mind. What happens to us as we experience life alters that state. I have found, through a return to the basics, that I'm not stuck in the altered state life has given me.

I have found pride in my jars of tomato soup. I have found pleasure in loaves of bread, fresh and hot, and more and more often, I'm processing the kitchen trash to the new location without the slightest distraction from my joy. As a result, I'm more open to laughter when the time comes.

Laughter won't swell up from worry, frustration, anger or disappointment, but it is exactly what we need to deal with these factors in our lives. We need to keep the path to laughter free and clear.

How do you deal with the garbage of your life? What's your 'natural' state of mind? Perhaps it is time to move the trash can.

That's What It's All About

You put your right foot in,
You put your right foot out;
You put your right foot in,
And you shake it all about.
You do the Hokey-Pokey,
And you turn yourself around.
That's what it's all about!

"Hokey pokey" was a slang term for ice cream in the 19th and early 20th centuries in several areas - including New York and parts of Great Britain - specifically for the ice cream sold by street vendors, or "hokey-pokey" men.

The song "The Hokey Pokey" was once titled "The Hokey Cokey." In 1940, during the Blitz in London, a Canadian officer suggested to Al Tabor, a British bandleader of the 1920s, 30s, and 40s that he write a party song to cheer the troops. The inspiration for the song's title, "The Hokey Pokey" came from an ice cream vendor whom Al had heard as a boy, calling out "Hokey pokey penny a lump. Have a lick, make you jump." He changed the name to "The Hokey Cokey" at the suggestion of the officer who said that 'hokey cokey', in Canada, meant 'crazy' and would sound better.

Written to create cheer and a better feeling for the population during the time of the war, the song was meant to inspire people to express themselves physically and celebrate living.

I once saw a bumper sticker that asked, "What if the Hokey Pokey really IS what it's all about?"

Well, I say it is.

At the core of simple living is the concept of enjoying the simple pleasures of the NOW. To focus all your talents on whatever task is at hand, give it your best and enjoy it. Writing, sewing, gardening, cooking, even brushing your teeth - if you focus on the task, learn to enjoy and perfect the process, then you have found the "groove" of life and living well.

The foundation of simple living is learning to enjoy and perfect the everyday motions of life. Isn't that what the Hokey Pokey is all about? Right foot, left foot, right hand, left hand, head—each in turn dipping in and out of the dance, and then just shaken about for good measure. Each line of the song focuses on a simple motion--pretty basic stuff. And yet, doing the Hokey Pokey will bring a smile to your face and joy to your heart, no matter what your age.

Try it. The "shake it all about" part is the most fun. It is almost impossible to shake it all about without at least cracking a smile.

We should live as though we're always dancing the Hokey Pokey. We should put all our pieces, parts, limbs, mind and efforts into living each moment of life to its fullest. Life is meant to be enjoyed.

The Hokey Pokey is about being all in, now, with what you've got. Each moment has the potential for joy. Find it. Look for it. Search in, out and all about for love, learning, or blessings. Learn the hokey pokey approach to life and you just might turn your life around.

And that's what it's all about.

May I Direct Your Attention

Ladies and Gentlemen! Allow me to direct your attention to high above the center ring!" This familiar instruction from the Master of Ceremonies at the circus would direct spotlights and the audience's eyes overhead, revealing the trapeze artists or the high wire daredevils smiling and waving in their sparkly outfits high above.

During the previous act, the audience watched clowns & trained elephants perform below, unaware of the performers gathering high above. And while our eyes are drawn above, someone is shoveling elephant dung in the darkness right in front of us. Performances, magic, media, manipulation - it is all about who directs our attention, and where we allow them to direct it. The way we use our attention shapes and controls our reality.

Whatever gets our attention gets our time and our lives. When we are attentive, we are absorbing, learning, growing... Our attention is like that circus spotlight - where it goes is how we grow. Whatever has our attention trains our minds. Whatever we light with our attention spotlight determines who we become. It affects how our brains work, how our minds grow, what we think, how we feel.

The fast pace of television, for example, trains your mind to lose interest in anything that doesn't travel at high speed. How many hours a day does the television have your attention? And how many times have you found yourself frustrated when dealing with something slow-moving?

And multi-tasking? A multitasking mind is inefficient, robbing you of the experience of being fully immersed in any one activity. Becoming fully immersed in an activity - so much that you lose yourself in it? Many people define that as "joy."

These days, American attentions are fragmented, to say the least. Rarely does any one thing get someone's full attention. It results in poor performance, poor quality, poor service, poor relationships, poor development. And although so many Americans seem to be desperate for attention, we rarely pay full attention to our own bodies, our own needs as human beings. That's why many spiritual and health practices encourage prayer, meditation, moments of quiet solitude. These moments are needed to pull our attention away from all the brainwashing the world puts in front of our attention - and focuses it back on what's important: our health and well-being.

Whatever has our attention is directly connected to who we are. Whatever has our attention has our spirit. And whatever has our spirit affects our soul.

The further we let our attention be drawn away from the goals, lessons, focus, needs that WE decide on, the more we can get tangled in the confusion of the world. The more we feel lost, disconnected, isolated. The more we grasp, the more we buy, the more we try to get the attention we so desperately crave from somewhere else.

Our attention is directly related to our power. This power determines who we are and what we become. If we don't take control of our attention, if we don't take control of our power, the world is full of folks willing to MIS-direct our attention and use our powers for their wishes. Like magicians and pickpockets, they create a stress or distraction that occupies our attention and gives them enough control to get away with our wallet, or impress us with cheap tricks.

You don't have to meditate, pray, or go off into the woods to regain control of your attention (although I've known all three of these to help). You can start by eliminating those attention-seeking things that obviously aren't worth your time. How many times are you going to dust that tacky shelf-sitter? How much time will you spend feeding the endless needs of a drama queen? How many hours will you spend watching television instead of learning something new, helping your child with homework, trying a new recipe? Where and how you spend your attention today determines what you will have and who you will become in the future.

We all can be distracted and misdirected. "If you stand for nothing, you'll fall for anything," so the saying goes. We need to direct our attention to what's important to us. Don't let others determine your life, just because you weren't paying attention where it was due.

Joy in a Parking Lot

Last week I stopped in at a department store to pick up toilet paper. As I crossed the parking lot on my way in, I passed an elderly lady with a cane, returning to her car. Toilet paper purchased, I returned to my car to discover that she was parked next to me. She was checking her pockets with one hand and trying to open her locked car door with her other.

"Did you lose your keys?" I asked.

She looked up, and nodded, "I know I had them,"

She kept checking the lower pockets in her jacket.

"You have another pocket, a breast pocket, on that jacket, did you check that one?" I asked.

She checked that pocket and found her keys.

"Bless your heart," she said, touching my arm.

We smiled at each other, having shared a brief moment of joy at the discovery of the keys.

Since returning to Central West Virginia eight years ago, Frank and I have tried to clear away a lot of the clutter of living to uncover some simple happiness and joy in our lives. We realized that, for us, the typical outlets for employment weren't conducive to this search, and we chose to start our home-based business and produce our magazine.

We still have clutter. We still have stress and struggles and challenges. But because we've cleared the air and have a desire to change our outlook in life, we're encountering more and more moments of joy. The trick is, when those moments do happen, to recognize them as a moment of joy, and to take the time to soak it in. If you rush through life looking to get more, make more, buy more, have more – you'll miss those moments.

Joy is helping a stranger find the keys in her pocket. Joy is kissing your spouse while cooking dinner together. Joy is your dog's tail wagging when you reach for the leash to go for a walk. Joy is a freezer full of venison and a pantry of home-canned vegetables and jelly. Joy is the fleeting moment when you have all the laundry washed, folded and put away.

Joy isn't out there, somewhere. It is in your life, every day if you simply catch it when it happens. It is there if you will just see it. There's a reason why you often hear about the "simple joys" in life. It's because joy in life IS simple. It's our notion that joy should be bigger, better or more advanced that makes it difficult for us to simply see.

I know when I first encountered the lady in the parking lot at the end of my day, I was tired, covered in newsprint ink smudges, wrinkled and grumpy about something. But because of that shared experience over the keys, I can't for the life of me remember what had upset me so. Whatever it was left my mind the moment her keys appeared. The reasons for my grumpiness became insignificant, and the warmth of her touch on my arm and the words she spoke became so significant that they touched my soul. I felt joy.

It isn't what we buy or what we have that brings us joy. We are all looking for a connection with others, our place and purpose in this world. It is in these discoveries that we find the joys of our life. Joy doesn't often arrive gift wrapped with an ornate bow. You might even find it in a parking lot.

What is Empathy? What is Love?

With the way things have been going in this country lately, it should come as no surprise that our nation is lacking in empathy and love. I have found research, studies that prove it. A long-running survey of the level of empathy in our nation shows a 40% drop in empathy over the last 37 years. Those of us who are older than 37 can surely say we have seen the effects of this decline.

But what is empathy? What is love? Ask ten different people, and you will get ten different answers. How can we understand what we are lacking if we don't understand what these terms mean? Empathy is the ability to understand and share the feelings of another without judgment. Can you see how a shortage of this ability ends up on your evening nightly news?

Love is the will to invest in someone or something else for your own or another's spiritual benefit. Perfect love is mutually beneficial. Love is not some indefinable emotion that makes us crazy. Love is an action, an investment in not only ourselves, but in others. Other people, pets, environments, communities.

I recently found myself in a discussion of tolerance among a group of people, one of whom kept flicking his cigarette butts on the sidewalk as he pontificated about the hatred that seems to have erupted in our culture. We discussed the roots of hatred; a lack of understanding, a lack of empathy, a lack of respect. Once he agreed with those as roots of hatred, I offered as an example, "Just as you hate the environment and the custodian."

Harsh? Perhaps. Accurate? Yes, I believe so. If hatred comes from a lack of empathy, a lack of understanding, a lack of respect, then every careless, thoughtless action we take can be another wave of suffering for someone or something else. Neglect is a lack of care, and without empathy (understanding others) and love (investing in others), we have become a nation of neglect. No wonder we find ourselves arguing over which lives matter.

Life matters. Love matters.

I myself am challenged by empathy. It's the "without judgment" part that gives me such a difficult time. I can sympathize, but sympathy looks down upon the "downtrodden." If we make judgments as we look down, we cannot truly understand and share the feelings of another, now can we? I have a hard time with difficult people, (which I suppose, likely makes me a difficult person in my own right). But, when I asked a wise woman how she deals with difficult people, she replied, "Bless them, then release them." In other words, extend love and empathy, and then move on. It is not up to us to judge, fix, or enlighten those we cannot find empathy for. For our own well-being, we can extend love to them, and then move on. We do not have to allow frustration, anger, hatred, grow within us.

How many of us dispense love as a reward, and not as an investment? How many of us actively love our community or the environment around us? There are those who believe our sole purpose on this earth is to love one another-to invest in one another for the greater good. Look at the community parks around you, most of them built or established fifty years ago. Look at the festivals that were established. Our parents and grandparents were people who loved their community.

After the terrible flooding in West Virginia (in 2016), I got hooked on the stories that came out of the recovering regions. They are all terrible and sad, but one story hit me hard. A couple, aware of the nearby creek, prepared for high water. They were responsible and caring for their animals, their vehicles, and moved and secured what they could. But it wasn't enough. They had to flee, and their beehives, chicken coop, home, cars, camper, were all underwater. Their hives and tens of thousands of bees were washed away, and their birds, secured in their coop, all drown. I thought of our beehives, our hens, our home, garden, all gone-and I sobbed. It is easy to judge those who live on the water. Why do they live there? Don't they pay attention when it rains? But like this couple, we live near water, and we know its typical behavior. I could not judge them for being naïve, or ignorant. I could not judge them for being unaware. I knew, like us, they tried to be responsible, tried to do all the right things, and still lost all. My sobbing was empathy. I could understand and feel her devastation because that loophole of judgment no longer kept me from feeling.

How sad that it takes such horrible events for us to also see love. Love as an investment. Love as an action. Neighbors helping neighbors; those with little donating time, money and supplies to those who have nothing. People investing in others' lives, other communities, in others' survival. When a tragedy takes away all you have, we see how important-and how effective-love is. When all else is washed away, love is what carries us through.

I am old enough to remember a time when this country had more empathy. A time when the word LOVE was on t-shirts, candles, hats, Frisbees. A time when the hit song rang out, "All you need is love." I remember when the term "trickledown economics" was hot, and talking money, love, or empathy—it seems like very little trickles down anymore.

This world needs more love, less judgment. Until then, we can have no empathy for each other, for the planet and the environment around us. Where do you invest your love? Facebook? Television? How harshly do you judge those you do not understand? When was the last time you actually felt the feelings of another?

Love is an action, and one we have to practice in all modes of our lives in order to have empathy in our lives and to nurture our collective spirits. There was a time when peace and love were trendy topics, a time when they were active elements in our society. It is time to activate them again.

Managing Transitions

transition - the process or a period of changing from one state or condition to another. synonyms: change, passage, move, transformation, conversion, metamorphosis, alteration, hand-over, changeover; segue, shift, switch, jump, leap, progression; progress, development, evolution, flux. transience - the state or fact of lasting only for a short time; the state or quality of passing with time or being ephemeral or fleeting.

Whenever I am highly stressed or unshakably blue, I try to remind myself, "This too, shall pass." Times of transition are especially stressful. Even celebrations and excitement are stressful on the body. Change, although we hate it, is often--but not always--a good thing. It's stressful, and it often takes time, so it is also drawn out and frustrating. It is an endurance run, not a sprint.

This year has been a personal period of transition. Add in the transitions we have seen this year in our nation, and I must tell you, I'm currently wound so tight I actually want to get on the rowing machine just to shake off all my excess jitters. My shoulder muscles are solid rocks. I try to shoulder boogie on my commute to work, just to work them loose.

Hey, I'm an overwhelmed, undervalued, stressed out, graduating, peri-menopausal woman who runs a business in the state ranked worst for businesses two years in a row. I consider myself highly unpredictable and potentially dangerous right now-mostly to myself--especially if I lose my notebook of lists that are currently helping me function. To-do lists, to-buy lists, to-pack lists, to-plan lists. Lists of things to not forget, lists of things to follow up with later. Homework, business work, library work. If I thought about it too hard, I might freak out. As it is, I feel a pan of brownies coming on.

I think about the current transitions I have in my life, and about the transitions happening in our communities, our state, our nation. Jinkies. No wonder I'm stressed.

I try to remember the rallies and the music of my youth: Love is the answer. Love is all we need. Joy to the world. Peace. Ohmmm. This too, shall pass.

Instead, I want to ram the back end of the 15-mile-per-hour log truck in front of me with my beat-up Subaru Impreza. I spend a good portion of each day trying to remember what I've forgotten because I've got that twangy panic feeling in my stomach. When I realize I just have too much to do, I think of things that comfort me: the love of family and friends, furry pets, full jars in the pantry. Letters from pen pals and well water. Free natural gas.

There are West Virginians, flooded out in July (2016), who are still without secure housing and heat. There are those who have no jars in their pantry. There are those who don't experience love or laughter on an everyday basis. And I complain about stress.

* * *

I remember once, hearing a news report on how the leaders in one of our enemy nations forbade music. No music. Anywhere. It stuck with me. What torture. What misery without music. Music soothes the savage beast, and excess stress sometimes feels like a beast inside me.

I have a friend who is fond of "furious dancing." In all my years knowing her, I have only seen her furious once, and perhaps her regular habit of dancing in her living room is why. She turns up her stereo and shimmies around on her plush throw rug and boogies on a regular basis. By the time I think of furious dancing, I'm often close to frazzled. I turn on my favorite get-the-butt-movin' songs, and I flap. I flail. I shake and jump and punch and kick and scare the dog and cat. When I'm finished, and I sit down panting and flushed, I do feel better, looser, less wound up. Of course, this all happens when Frank isn't home. It just doesn't work as well with someone watching. They might think you are having some kind of fit or attack. Of course, if I danced on a regular basis, I might be able to calm my moves enough to dance with my husband. Wouldn't that be nice?

A transition is a metamorphosis, a transformation from one thing to another. A jump into a different mindset, a leap of faith that this evolution is progress. I think of butterflies hatching from cocoons, chicks hatching from eggs. It is a difficult, strenuous, rather drawn-out fight. I imagine they are mentally stressed as well.

Exercise, music, lists. These are the tools I use to manage transitional periods. I imagine butterflies have the music of nature and chicks have their families to encourage and soothe them too. When all else fails to loosen me up, I'll take Daisy out for a brisk walk. Well, she's fat and not so brisk anymore, but the air is brisk and fresh, and even though winter has come, the woods are still filled with sounds. Woodpeckers. Crunching leaves. Wind.

With the presidential campaign, the election, fires, floods, standoffs, riots, this year has been a rough year for all of us. It is difficult to share and spread love when you are so stressed and frustrated, and our state and our nation is full of stressed and frustrated folks right now. And with dark falling so early in the evening? I could grump my way clear through until spring. But my husband would not appreciate it, nor my students, nor our patrons at the library. What do you do to relieve your stress? Dance? Row? Sing? Party with friends? Hop in a hot tub? Walk in the snow? When was the last time you did it?

Why Be Fine, When You Can Be Fantastic?

Winter is my least favorite time of year. Shut in, stuck without the highlights of spring, summer, and fall. Except for hawk screeches, or coyote calls, the outside world becomes quiet. The skies are gray, the yard is muddy, and those bed covers are harder to toss back in the morning.

I've heard several folks mention lately that "they aren't themselves," or they have a case of the blahs. People pause more before answering, "How are you," as though they must give it some thought first. Folks who typically answer, "I'm good" come back with a quiet, "I'm okay," or "I've been better."

I once worked with a corporation president in Chicago whom I called, "Mr. Wonderful." I watched him struggle often with the challenges of the business, but no matter what, when asked how he was, he replied, "I'm wooonderful!" Never did I hear him say, "I'm fine," or "I've been better." He knew it was important (in a company selling toys and magic tricks), that cheer was part of his brand.

The truth is, everybody's got something challenging their happiness. Every person you encounter has a worry, even Mr. Wonderful. Every person you speak with has at least one challenge in their life, often six or ten or more. That grumpy cashier may have had an argument with her teenager before work. That neighbor who cut you short may be running late for a meeting because he had a flat tire that morning and had to change it in the cold winter wind.

Some folks keep their problems to themselves, while others tell their sad tale to the world. Either way, everybody has something. In proper perspective, our problems are no bigger, worse, or heavier than anyone else's. And while it may seem there are those who have fewer burdens than our own, there are certainly millions who have as many, or even more problems. What right do we have to dump our burdens on them?

It takes ten positive comments to outweigh one negative. Too often we get caught up with the negative opinions, attitudes, actions, and thoughts of those around us and on television--creating a negative lifestyle that leaves us unhappy, depressed, hopeless and angry. In order to avoid this and move from a negative lifestyle to a positive lifestyle--we need to begin changing the way we see circumstances and change the way we interact with each other and the world.

Mr. Wonderful knew the power of positive thinking. He never let a bad morning ruin his day or his week. He knew that every time he claimed to be "wooonderful," he was combating, and surviving the negatives of his days. Every time he said he was wonderful, his mind heard him, and took it to heart.

Our words determine our mindset. Although I am prone to answer "How are you?" with "fine" (whether I'm fine or not), I am trying to change that habit to respond with, "I'm fantastic!" If I say or hear it ten times a day, I've knocked out the effects of ONE negative I've encountered. I've made one more step toward getting balance in my life.

Another friend answers the obligatory "how are you" with "Oh, I'm hangin' in there." He may not be wonderful, but he's surviving and overcoming. Sometimes, that's the best we can hope for. Other times, instead of just hangin', we could hope to be swinging through the trees. Answer "how are you" just once with, "I'm swingin' through the trees." See if that doesn't just lift your spirits.

Everybody's got somethin'. We may feel our problems are so immense and unique, we are excused from our obligation to life and society. But we are responsible for our own happiness, and anything worth having takes work. Everyone has problems, but only those who have learned not to dwell on them are happy.

We need to continually encourage ourselves and to encourage others. There are too many unhappy people in this world who spend time and effort in the other direction. There are those who feel we should all be unhappy if they are unhappy. Unhappiness is an epidemic in our country, and every empowering word we speak is a volley in the battle for joy.

We are conditioned not to tout our blessings. Conditioned not to be boastful or proud. But it is common practice to "sing the blues" and even try to "outdo" each other by noting our burdens are greater. We've all done it--heard a sob story and responded with one of our own. Like comparing scars, we present our problems as though they were medals—battles we have survived. No wonder we are a miserable society. (We can wallow in this mud of life or stand up and walk out of it. Which would you rather do?)

The world is burdened enough. The human condition, alone, is a struggle. Winters are enough of a challenge, the time of year when we often battle these blues. Don't just "hang in there." Remember, in perspective, your life is full of blessings. You are wonderful, great, fantastic! With a mental image and a few words, you could even be swinging through the trees.

And if that doesn't work, break out the seed catalogs. Spring isn't too far away.

Burdens and Blessings

Life is a series of burdens and blessings. Unfortunately, both cause stress and anxiety. You can be dealt one, then the other, then back again, a million times a day. The trick is to learn to just roll with it – and hope the burdens don't outweigh the blessings. I believe you have to count them both to survive.....

Last year, Frank and I were blessed with a new (to us) vehicle (blessing). Frank was not "going to work" (burden) but instead, farmed at home (burden/blessing), and could piddle around the roads in our beat-up Ford pick-up truck (blessing). His back had been ailing him (burden), but visits to the chiropractor were helping (blessing).

With that situation, we decided to sell our old van (burden). It was my father's (blessing) but had 400,000-plus miles and a rusty body (burden) and just sat in the yard (burden). We listed it in all the trader's mags, and people came and went and called to see it (burden), and never did buy (burden).

Then Frank went back to work (blessing), and we didn't feel so pressured to sell the van (blessing). He no longer carried his wallet in his pocket when driving (which helps keep his back aligned), and he felt better (blessing). He was working again without extreme pain (blessing).

Two weeks after he'd been trekking back and forth to Glenville, the Ford truck broke down (burden). But, we still had the van (now a blessing) so we parked the truck for expensive repair (burden) and both of us worked (blessing), preparing on the sidelines for the upcoming annual family reunion (blessing). Close to 125 people (blessing), expected at our house (uh, burden).

So, two days before the reunion, we pile in the van to go pick up extra tables and chairs for the event (burden). On the way, the van breaks down (burden), right in front of our friend's house (blessing), who was home (blessing), but doesn't have a phone (burden).

We both had to work the next day (now a burden), still had to pick up tables and chairs (burden), and we only had one operating vehicle (burden), which was somewhere where we weren't (burden), and wouldn't hold all the tables and chairs (burden).

However, we had just enough time (blessing) to get a ride to our house, call to find a part, (which was affordable – blessing), get in the new-to-us ride (blessing) and fly to the parts store in Spencer who had it in stock (blessing.) While Frank was on the phone with the parts store, I took out my wallet to show our friend (blessing), who gave us a ride home (blessing), a picture of my niece (blessing) and her unborn jelly bean who will be a boy (blessing).

Meanwhile, another family member, Bob, whose vehicle went down the previous month (burden), had a new (to him) vehicle in his driveway (blessing), but the paperwork to make it legal hadn't been processed yet by the state (burden). Bob, after work that day, knew we were supposed to pick up chairs and tables (burden), so he had his ride drop him off at the table and chair location, thinking we could give him a ride the rest of the way home (thinking – a blessing.)

We were pulling out of the driveway to head to the parts store, when in pulls a helpful friend in a truck (blessing) - pulling the non-operating vehicle (burden) of a second family member, Alex, who had been sitting, broken down, on the far side of Sand Ridge Hill (burden) for more than an hour.

But, Alex's vehicle is an easy fix as well (blessing), and an affordable part (blessing) and guess what – we're just now on our way to the parts store (blessing).

So, on a quest for two parts (burden), we fly towards Spencer, not knowing Bob is waiting for us to pick him up with the tables and chairs (known and unknown burdens). We arrive in the parking lot with twenty minutes to spare (blessing).

We can fix our van tonight (blessing), get tables and chairs in time after work tomorrow (maybe), get Alex's vehicle back on the road more quickly (blessing), and both still make it to work in the morning without issue (blessing). Right?

Frank reached to the console for his wallet - which was still in the van, broken down, in front of our friend's house.

I reached then for my wallet - which was still on the kitchen counter where I showed my friend my niece's picture before we left in a rush.

!!!

I am happy to report that neither of us spontaneously combusted that evening in the parking lot of Advance Auto Parts in Spencer (blessing). In fact, we both just sat, beaten and defeated (burden), thinking that life had decided we were going to be dealt a lot of crap that day (burden), we were not going to be ready for the reunion (burden), and there was just nothing we could do about it (burden).

As I lowered my head to wallow in misery, I spied the money bag I had used that day to collect on my newspaper delivery run. Within it was just enough cash to cover what we needed.

(Blessed Miracle!)

Meanwhile, 40 miles away, a third family member, Jim, with a truck (blessing) encountered Bob's original ride home (blessing). Jim, who knew we were one vehicle down and in Spencer (burden), headed towards Bob and the tables and chairs (blessing).

So, we head back from Spencer in our working vehicle (blessing), to the broken van (burden), which Frank can easily fix (blessing), now in the dark (burden), across from a friend's house (blessing), who has flashlights (blessing) with dead batteries (burden), but just fixed a big dinner (blessing).

Frank fixed the van (blessing) and while we were on the porch eating hot dogs (blessing), we plan how we can pick up chairs and tables (burden), still ignorant that Bob was counting on us for a ride. (Actually, it is a blessing that we didn't know, or the added pressure may have caused a mental meltdown).

Then up pulled Jim with Bob, in a truck with a bed full of tables and chairs (blessing, blessing, blessing).

Bob, who hadn't had dinner (burden), and waited two hours for a ride (burden), was also fed by our friends (blessing).

So, before too late that evening (blessing), we had all vehicles operating (blessing), and all family members home (blessing), all family members fed (blessing), and tables and chairs unloaded (blessing). We were ready for the reunion (blessing), and we both had vehicles (blessing) to get us to work (blessing) the next day.

(WHEW!)

Anyone who says life isn't a roller coaster ride isn't counting all the highs (blessings) or lows (burdens). The best you can do is roll along, laugh when you can, grit your teeth when you can't, and occasionally throw your hands in the air - all without throwing up.

Hopefully, at the end of the day, the blessings will outnumber the burdens.

And that, in itself, is a blessing.

About the Author:

Lisa Hayes-Minney self-published her first book when she was 12 years old, producing a single issue with father's typewriter and mother's sewing machine. The inside pages were hand-illustrated in pen and crayon; the outside cover was made from carboard stock covered in fabric from an old feed sack decorated with vinyl lettering.

Lisa has been writing professionally for over 25 years. She has been a copywriter, content producer, newspaper reporter, newspaper and magazine columnist, magazine publisher, AmeriCorps volunteer, and college professor. She now serves as director of a small, rural, public library and operates her own business, Stumptown Publishing, LLC.

Lisa has a B.A. in Written English with a minor in Journalism, and an M.F.A. in Creative Writing. She has received awards from the West Virginia Press Association, West Virginia Writer's Inc., and Parkersburg Area Community Foundation. Her work has been included in *Wonderful West Virginia Magazine*, *The Hur Herald*, *The Trillium*, *The Charleston Anvil*, *Entropy Magazine*, *GreenPrints Magazine*, *Memoir Magazine,* and has also been included in Mountains Upon Mountains: New Appalachian Nature Writing (from West Virginia University Press), Empathy in Art: Embracing the Other (from WritingForPeace.org), and Feminine Rising: Voices of Power & Invisibility (from Cynren Press).

For more than a decade, Lisa served as the publisher of *Two-Lane Livin' Magazine*, a free monthly publication featuring regular columns relating to rural, simple, sustainable living in West Virginia. This collection includes forty-one of Lisa's favorites from 123 installments she wrote, written throughout the run of the magazine.

This is the ninth book Lisa has published in her lifetime, including the first, Just A Simple Life, the story of a mouse who lived in a public junior high school. Others include two books on magic tricks ghost written and created for Fun, Incorporated; Favorite Reflections, a collection of her columns from four years as a newspaper columnist at *The Calhoun Chronicle*; Thus Far, a collection of her poetry written before turning 40; and two region-specific Christmas Samplers featuring historical Christmas tales and articles from local newspaper files.

Lisa distributes a seasonal email newsletter that provides updates on her projects, links to newly published work, information relating to libraries and writing, and web new services from Stumptown Publishing. To sign up for the newsletter or for more information, visit http://www.lhayesminney.net.

www.ingramcontent.com/pod-product-compliance
Ingram Content Group UK Ltd.
Pitfield, Milton Keynes, MK11 3LW, UK
UKHW041936190726
13854UKWH00004B/1629